WE ARE
NOT
AFRAID

#1 *New York Times* Bestselling Author
HOMER HICKAM

WE ARE NOT AFRAID

Strength and Courage from the Town That Inspired the #1 Bestseller and Award-Winning Movie *October Sky*

Health Communications, Inc.
Deerfield Beach, Florida

www.bci-online.com
www.chickensoup.com

TEEN
B
HiCKAM, HOMER

Library of Congress Cataloging-in-Publication Data

Cataloging-in-Publication Data is available from the Library of Congress.

©2002 Homer Hickam
ISBN 0-7573-0012-X (trade paper)

Publisher: Health Communications, Inc.
3201 S.W. 15th Street
Deerfield Beach, FL 33442-8190

Cover and chapter title-page design by Lisa Camp
Inside book formatting by Dawn Grove

To Master Sergeant Joe Alderman,
U.S. Army Special Forces,
who was never afraid, and to
Mrs. Linda Holder Alderman, who still isn't.

Contents

Acknowledgments

This book is, in many respects, a letter of thanks to the people of the United States of America. Because of their willingness to fight for freedom, I was given the opportunity to grow up in a peaceful, prosperous land and receive a wonderful education. For their courage and constant vigilance against oppression, I am eternally grateful.

A personal note of gratitude is also due to the citizens of Coalwood, West Virginia. The men and women who built my hometown and kept it going, and now seek to restore it, are true heroes. There are too many of them to list, but I hope they all know how much I appreciate what they've done and continue to do for me. I am also indebted to all the West Virginians who sent me their stories of strength and inspiration. They were wonderful stories and I wish I could have included all of them in this work.

Very special thanks goes to Frank Weimann, my literary agent in New York, who practically insisted that I write this book, believing it was the right book at the right time to help Americans through these perilous times. My appreciation is also extended to Peter Vegso, publisher of Health Communications, Inc., whose enthusiasm and support convinced me to go ahead with the work. Christine Belleris and Allison Janse, my HCI editors, have been amazingly responsive and perfectly attuned to what I wanted to accomplish. Kim Weiss, HCI director of communications, has done a remarkable job of promoting this work in a very short time. In fact, I am awed by the professionalism of everyone at HCI, a truly great publishing house. My motion picture/television/literary agent Mickey Freiberg has also continued his wonderful support for all my projects, including this one.

On the home front, appreciation and love is sent to Linda Terry Hickam, my wife, first editor and assistant, who always improves my work and supports me every day with Web site and mail chores, scheduling, and a thousand other things. I couldn't do my work without her. I'd like to also thank Homer H. Hickam Sr., my dad, the finest man I have ever known. I just wish he was around to read this and all my books. Of course, appreciation must go to my mom, Elsie Lavender Hickam. She still typifies the spirit of Coalwood's women, proud and tenacious, and she also managed to raise a pretty good crop of children. I was privileged to be one of them.

Why You Should Read This Book

In today's world, fear seems to be everywhere. Sometimes it's an immediate fear caused by a sense of imminent danger. When terrible things happen before our eyes, instant fear is a normal reaction. Our minds are designed to dredge up fear in such times so that adrenaline will spurt through our veins and our heart rates will speed up. That gets us ready to escape or fight. This is a good, rational kind of fear that is meant to be temporary and get us past an immediate crisis.

The problem is that there are so many folks in the world today who are always afraid. This was true even before the atrocities of September 11, 2001. Along with fear, dread also seems to have gained a foothold everywhere. Dread is the little voice that keeps whispering to us about all the bad things that might happen. When a constant sense of dread takes over, people start to avoid doing much of anything. It becomes a habit. They're afraid to fly, to travel, to take new jobs, to consider new concepts and ideas. Everyday challenges of life become too much to handle. The joy of living is lost to despair.

At the beginning of the twenty-first century, there is little doubt that we Americans live in perilous times. We have real enemies who wish us ill. In fact, some of them would like to kill us and have said so, out loud and in no uncertain terms. That's pretty scary. We also live in an ever-changing world that is often unpleasant and hard to understand. The economy goes from dizzying heights to recession for no reason we can discern, new diseases threaten that can't be cured, politicians manipulate and control us, and our scientists go too far and too fast. Every day, it seems some kind of craziness assaults us. As rational beings, we start to think maybe it would be best to just hunker down and pull the blankets over our heads. Life seems too dangerous and frightening to enjoy. We wonder if we'll ever be happy again. This is the kind of thinking that makes us wide open to letting fear and dread take over our lives.

Dread and fear are really a nasty pair. Once they become a habit, they can be difficult to beat. A lot of times people fall into the habits of fear and dread without even realizing it. Self-pity, being negative, timidity or constant worry are all symptoms of being afraid. So is an inability to hold a family together. There is plenty of speculation as to why so many people have become habitually fearful, not just of war or terrorism or disease, but of simply living. Some say it's because of a pervasive media that constantly bombards us with stories of pain and suffering and evil. Or maybe it's because our new Internet society cuts us off from the realities of life, both good and bad. From wherever it comes, there is no doubt fear is persistent in our land and dread a constant whisper. People have become hooked on being afraid.

If you want to stop being afraid, or if you want to avoid the habits of fear and dread, this book can help by teaching you a philosophy of life that will fill your heart and soul with a sense of well-being and confidence. It is a philosophy that was developed by real people who led good, happy and hearty lives while managing to raise a crop of children who went on to have successful lives of their own. The people who developed and lived this fear-destroying philosophy were the people who raised me. As their example and teachings helped me to be strong and unafraid, my accounts of who they were and what they did can also help you to beat fear and keep dread on the run. They can be the model for the rest of your life.

A few years ago, I wrote about growing up in the little mining town of Coalwood, West Virginia, in a book titled *Rocket Boys*. It was a huge success, and Universal Studios made a popular movie based on it, calling the film *October Sky*. Since then, *Rocket Boys* (its mass-market version is also titled *October Sky*) has sold nearly a million copies. I followed *Rocket Boys* with two more bestselling books about life in Coalwood, *The Coalwood Way* and *Sky of Stone*. These form what I call the Coalwood trilogy.

When I wrote my books about Coalwood, I only hoped to write good stories to entertain my readers. But since their publication and the making of the movie, I have been humbled by thousands of heartfelt letters and e-mails from people around the world thanking me for the inspiration they've received. I am humbled, mainly because the stories I told reflect not my wisdom but that of the Coalwood of my youth. I am simply the voice of the people who raised me.

Because so many people admire my books and the movie *October Sky*, I am one of the most requested speakers in the country. After the September 11 terrorist attacks, I sensed a need from audiences to hear about the brave people of my hometown and how they taught me lessons of strength and courage. As a result, hundreds of people came up to me after my speeches and said my stories had helped them work past their fears. They even showed me their notes! Nearly all of them also said I should write a book, one based on the beliefs and attitudes of the people who raised me.

I am not a philosopher. I have no academic degrees in either psychology, or sociology or any other kind of -ology. But I was raised by a wise and steady and strong people who tested their approach to life during good times and bad. It is their wisdom I have to give, not my own. That is why I decided to write this book—so that everyone can have access to their philosophy. Their attitudes sustained them and let them live full, happy lives without fear or dread. Adopting their attitudes as your own can do the same for you. That's why you should read this book.

What was it about Coalwood that caused the development of a way of life that defeated fear? The Coalwood I write about was the one I knew when I was a boy growing up in the 1940s and 1950s. During that time, it might be fairly said that the town always lived during perilous times. At its center sat a deep coal mine, one entered by going straight down a long, narrow, vertical shaft that dropped nearly a thousand feet. It was a dangerous mine that could quickly fill with explosive methane gas and its roof was a jumble of razor-edged rock. Every day, the men of Coalwood entered that mine to dig out coal, an inherently risky proposition. That required courage, but not the kind that men can show in an instant. Coalwood's miners had to figure out how to be brave over a long period of time. The same was true for Coalwood's women. Every day, they sent their husbands off to work the deep coal, knowing very well they might not ever see them again. It is impossible to do that year after year without developing a philosophy of life that defeats fear and puts aside the feelings of constant dread. Coalwood's people figured out how to stop being afraid over the long haul, and this is the wisdom this book seeks to give its readers.

There are a few other things that should be understood about my hometown so that its wisdom makes more sense. During most of its existence, Coalwood was a pure company town. That meant not only the mine was owned by the company but so was everything else—*everything!* The houses we lived in were company-owned. The company built the roads and the fences. All the stores were company stores. All the adult men in Coalwood worked for the company. The doctor and dentist were company men, their services provided free. The preachers were also company men and since the churches were company-owned, we liked to say we got the low-bid religion. We said that with a grin. Our religion was of our souls and our hearts and our minds, not of any particular denomination. But the point I'm making is that Coalwood and its people were one and the same. The knowledge that everyone is working toward the same goal is very powerful. It can provide tremendous strength and support.

The adult women of Coalwood were either married to

company men or were teachers at the Coalwood School. The men of the town had a job, that of mining out the coal, but the women had what was considered a more important job, that of keeping the family together and caring for the children, *all* of the children. Every adult woman in town could, if the situation warranted it, apply her hand to the backside of a wayward child, even if the child didn't belong to her, in order to give immediate guidance in the correct path of personal behavior. The women in town were pretty much unified in what that correct path was supposed to be. As a boy prone to more than a little mischief, I got small love taps on my posterior from time to time that transmitted that information very well! The women never hurt me, not once, but it was just a perfectly applied light swat that got my attention in a positive way.

For some reason, my life in Coalwood was often spent as an observer. It was as if from my earliest reckoning of where I lived, I knew I was in a special place and needed to record it. In 1949, when I was in the second grade, I started my own newspaper to write down all that I could see. My friend Roy Lee Cooke joined me in my little enterprise, which I called, perhaps not creatively but at least accurately, *The Coalwood News*. Roy Lee and I scoured the town for stories and then laboriously hand-printed each paper, for which we charged a nickel. We always sold out. Our stories tended toward the personal, and that perhaps was the reason for their popularity. If we saw a lady at the company store, for instance, we followed her around and wrote down everything she bought, including the SSS tonic the missus thought might be just the thing to perk up her husband's romantic inclinations. If we saw a man lolling around on the post office steps chewing tobacco and then observed his wife out tending the vegetable garden, we jotted that down, too, wondering in print why one was lolling and chewing while the other was working? We pretty much stuck our noses into everybody's business, and that meant everybody loved our little newspaper except maybe the folks who found themselves in it. There were a lot of complaints sent sailing over the gossip fence in the direction of my mother, hoping she would shut our little news sheet down.

Mom resisted the demands for the extinction of *The Coalwood News* until I wrote about a lady who fell down in the creek and got her behind pinched by a big, mad crawl-dad. I especially liked the way I described the little dance she did, crow-hopping up on the creek bank and spinning around like a top. It was that story that went beyond even my mom's liberal attitude toward the press since the lady doing the crow-hopping was Elsie Lavender Hickam, my mother herself. My First Amendment rights in Coalwood were completely and utterly suspended for the remainder of time or the extinction of the universe, whichever came last. But I kept observing the attitudes of my people and learning from them. I still do.

The Coalwood I write about was the town I knew growing up, from my birth in 1943 until I left to go into the army in 1966. I was part of a generation who benefited from the earned wisdom of a great people who inspired their children to also be great. As a Coalwood boy, I came to understand at a very early age that God had determined that there was no joy greater than hard work, and he made no water holier than the sweat off one's brow; but I also understood that love is God's gift to us that we might share it, and it is also the ache in our soul if it might be lost. The people of Coalwood faced each day the dangers of the coal mine and the isolation of the mountains. To survive and to have a good life demanded living in a simple and realistic way. There could be no pretending that their world was anything but hard and arduous and often filled with danger. This understanding of the fundamental nature of life resulted in a practical, no-nonsense, yet often humor-filled, approach to living that got them through the worst of times with an almost unnatural resilience and a special kind of fortitude. Over a lifetime, they learned to take on these attitudes:

> *We are proud of who we are.*
> *We stand up for what we believe.*
> *We keep our families together.*
> *We trust in God but rely on ourselves.*

These attitudes were summed up by a singular assumption. It was an assumption that was as normal to the people of Coalwood as breathing. They always seemed to be saying it, not out loud but in the manner in which they took on every challenge and every danger that came their way:

> *We are not afraid.*

In the following pages, I will explain how each attitude worked to give the people of my hometown a happy, fearless life. Since I'm essentially a storyteller, I'll tell stories to illustrate how Coalwood's people taught their children and each other to live with strength and courage and dignity. In "Other Voices," I will include stories written by others who grew up in Coalwood or nearby. As you get to know the people who raised me, I hope that you will come to understand their attitudes toward life and adopt them as your own. If you do, I am confident you will join the good people of my hometown and say, believe and assume, no matter what may come your way:

We are not afraid.

The Coalwood Attitudes of Strength and Courage

We are proud of who we are.
We stand up for what we believe.
We keep our families together.
We trust in God but rely on ourselves.

The Coalwood Assumption:

We are not afraid.

#1

We are proud of who we are.

The people who built Coalwood and the other southern West Virginia mining towns in the early twentieth century found themselves in a beautiful but essentially inhospitable place. It was an area that had never before been settled by human beings and for good reason. It was clogged with steep, rock-strewn, deeply forested hills that were unsuitable to farming or raising herds of animals. There was hardly any flat land at all, and the mountains were so close, only a thin sliver of sky could be seen between them. Its narrow hollows were prone to floods, and nearly every spring a great wall of water came sweeping down one of them, taking away everything in its path. Long, dry summers produced forest fires that would sweep over the ridges and roar down into the valleys like giant fireballs. For a hundred miles in any direction, there were plenty of better places to live.

Pre-Columbian Americans only used the area for occasional hunting forays, and American pioneers like Daniel Boone mostly bypassed the area to get to Kentucky or points south and west. For centuries, southern West Virginia remained isolated and wild. When people did finally come to live there in significant numbers, they came to mine coal, a perilous enterprise. Yet, every day in all the years I observed them, the men of Coalwood, perfectly aware of all the dangers in the place where they worked, emerged from their misty hollows and walked to the mine as if they didn't have a care in the world. I was always comforted by the sound of the tromp of their boots as they walked to the mine, the low murmur of their pleasant voices and the occasional whistling of cheerful tunes. When I looked out on that long line of men with their bobbing helmets, they looked for all the world like soldiers going into combat. And, in a very real way, they were. They were company men, warriors against a common foe, confident and certain of who they were and why they were going to work. They worked as a team, and each man depended on the other. If one of them made a mistake, all of them paid a terrible price. The police and firemen who raced inside the burning Twin Towers in New York on September 11, 2001, remind me of Coalwood men. They were the same kind of people, going with confidence to work in a place of peril for the greater good of the community.

I am certain that the children of those policemen and firemen are proud of their parents and their sacrifice. It is right and proper that they are. In the same way, I am proud of the men and women who raised me and my friends. I am proud because they taught me to be proud. The people of Coalwood thought it vastly important that their children understand who they were and take pride in that knowledge. It was a fundamental attitude, one that connected them to the town and also, paradoxically, would allow them to confidently leave it. Our parents were quite well aware that most of the outside world considered them to be quaint, uneducated hillbillies with a culture to match. With that in mind, they knew their children would need to go out into that world equipped with not only a good education but a belief and pride in themselves.

Although our parents and teachers wanted to make certain we knew about our town, sometimes outsiders saw us better than we saw ourselves. One of my favorite "older" boys in Coalwood was Bill Todd. I always admired him. Tall, self-assured, he lived just a couple of houses down from our house on Tipple Row. He studied hard, made good grades and eventually went off to college. Years later, his wife Phyllis captured Coalwood perfectly in this letter she sent to me:

> *I am not a "Coalwood girl" but it was there, visiting Bill's family and friends, that the door to an entirely different world was opened to me. Meticulously manicured lawns and flower beds ablaze with colors of the seasons were commonplace . . . not a scrap of litter to be seen anywhere. Snow-white houses had front porches where hanging flower baskets were in abundance. Cheerfully colored porch furniture was filled with visiting neighbors. The beautiful community church was the center focus of the town. On Sunday mornings the congregation was always dressed in their "Sunday best." The men usually wore dark suits, and the women always wore hats, gloves and a purse.*
>
> *Coal mining was ever-present in the lives of Coalwood residents. It was hard and dirty work. Those who grew up in Coalwood perhaps do not recognize how strongly the good morals, strong values, tenacious*

*work ethic and social graces shown by the people of the
community impressed those of us not privileged to have
lived in that town. . . .*

Phyllis Todd wrote the truth. Coalwood was a special
place, and it had gotten that way by hard work and tough
attitudes toward life and a belief in the way people should
live. Adults in Coalwood taught their children to be proud of
the Coalwood way of life. The use of stories was one of
the most important ways to do that. Parents talked about
those who had come before, of grandparents and great-
grandparents and uncles and aunts and cousins. They told
sad and grand and funny stories of the past to their children,
usually around the kitchen table. We children listened and in
turn passed those stories on to our friends. We could see the
way the stories interweaved with one another, and we understood that we had a common history. We were proud
because they were stories that had been given to us as something important that we needed to know.

Every human being on this planet has been afraid at one
time or another. That certainly includes me. But fear has
never ruled me, and I believe the reason is that I have never
been alone in any battle, even when I stood completely,
utterly, physically by myself. No matter where I've been,
whether in the mud and bush of Vietnam, or in a cold, murky
river trying to rescue people in a sunken ship, or standing in
front of a critical audience of astronauts in an attempt to
sway them to my opinion, I have never felt alone. I have
always been surrounded by the people who raised me.
Forever and always, the people of Coalwood are with me,

their hands holding mine, their strong arms lifting me up, their voices whispering:

We are proud of who we are.
We are not afraid.

To defeat fear, it is necessary to be confident of who you are and rooted to something of substance, something larger than yourself. The people of Coalwood knew that instinctively. My parents liked to sit around the kitchen table after supper and talk of the events of the day, and after my father had related all the gossip of the coal mine, and my mother had filled him in on her doings, they would begin to tell tales of the past, theirs and Coalwood's. I always stayed to listen and sat with my elbows propped on the table, my chin in my hands and my mind filled with the rich imaginings of times gone by. Through their own words, I saw my parents as they were before I was born, and it allowed me to understand why they sometimes did inexplicable things, why they thought something was funny, or sad, or important. I loved that part of the day when, through their stories, my parents came to be more than my parents but also young people, just like me, with hopes, dreams and the courage to do things. Sometimes they made me laugh. Sometimes I felt like crying because I was so sad about something that had happened to them. But, in the end, I was mostly proud. If they hadn't told those stories, I would have never truly known them or been connected to them in the same way.

What does this mean to you? If there is anything more likely to cause fear, it's a sense of being incomplete and detached from society. To be confident, it is necessary to know the vast trail of people and circumstances who made you, whether it is your individual family, town or country. The primary thing is to become connected with something larger than yourself, something good and wholesome and productive and grand. If you're an adult, perhaps too late to hear stories directly from your parents or from those who raised you, it is never too late to know the history of the people from who you came and the country in which you live. History is the great time machine, the means of traveling back to understand the fundamental foundations on which we stand and the path on which our ancestors trod to get where we are now. To know the path before us, it is necessary to know the path behind.

One thing to always remember: You are a masterpiece, the result of billions of possibilities. The odds against you existing as a person, when you stop to think about it, are unimaginable. All the events in the history of the universe and the world, all the animals and people that came together, everything that has ever happened had to happen pretty much exactly as it did in order for you to exist. Do you think that's just an accident? It isn't. You exist for a purpose. Never doubt it. You exist for a goal that the Maker of the Universe has set for you. You exist so that the world might be a better place. And you also exist so that you might be happy.

When the atrocities happened on September 11, 2001, my mom's reaction was to wonder about the men who had done it. "Who were their people?" she asked. Coalwoodians asked that a lot of strangers, and especially about the boys their daughters brought home to meet the folks. They wanted to know everything they could about that boy, but mostly they wanted to know: *Who were their people?* Knowing somebody's people can tell you a lot, although not necessarily everything.

In the last few decades, there has been an emphasis on teaching what is wrong with the United States and the errors of its founding fathers and its people during its trying pioneer days. Popular entertainment has also focused on the ills of our history. Time and again, our history has been presented to us as shameful. This focus on the negatives of our past is the result of haughty hindsight, as if we from our comfortable, electrified homes might have done things differently and with more morality than people with hungry families to feed who faced a huge, raw and dangerous continent. It is part of being an American, of course, to know the truth, even when it is an ugly truth. But before the negative aspects of our history are taught, we need first to know the stories of the courage and undaunting optimism of the people who made us into the greatest and most giving country the world has ever known.

Although I write in this book mostly of Coalwood, I am proud to be an American. The United States of America is a great country, a compassionate country, a country filled with unbridled charity. We feed starving people across the globe. Our way of governing ourselves is the hope and the example for a fearful world filled with dictators and tyrants. If you're an American, you should be proud, and you should do everything you can to glorify and honor your country's past while trying to improve its present so that its future will be even better. You should make up your mind right now to never listen to those who would run our nation down because of their bitter perception of our past and who we are. We've been wrong, terribly wrong, but we have always triumphed over the ills of our society, whether it be slavery or economic depression or war or terrorist assault. We live amongst a compassionate and optimistic people striving to do good. You are an American. There is nothing more that you can say that should make you any prouder. As an American, you also have a duty to be happy. It says right there in our Declaration of Independence that we have God-given rights to life, liberty and the pursuit of happiness. So do your duty. Learn how to be happy and keep this in mind: You can't be happy unless you stop being afraid.

To be unafraid, you must be connected to something larger than yourself, and it needs to be something good and fine. But there is something more you need to do. You need to tell stories and you need to listen to them, too. Stories are how you will learn who you are and become connected to the strength all of us need to survive and prosper in the world today. If you are a parent, or an adult in a family with children, remember your responsibility to let children know who they are. They need to be rooted in the firm substance of family and country and be proud of it. Tell your stories to your children. Think long and hard of the events of your past, or your parents' past, of your Uncle Joe's or Aunt Maria's, and of the heroes who built this country. Form the story in your mind with a beginning, middle and end, then tell it with all the enthusiasm you can muster. You will find, without fail, that you actually know many stories of yourself and your family that will be filled with heroism and glory and even low comedy. It almost doesn't matter. Just remember to tell your stories in such a way that after you finish, you and the children who have heard them might say, if only in a whisper:

We are proud of who we are.
We are not afraid.

WE KNOW OUR HISTORY

The habit that is fear and dread can be compared to having a chronic disease. Some of us have gotten so used to having it, we don't even know we're infected. A symptom of this disease is that we walk around with slumped shoulders and drag one heavy foot after another. We dread getting out of bed in the morning, certain that only awful things are going to happen when we do. We never have anything good to say about anything, and that includes ourselves. We don't like the way we look. We feel victimized. We're envious of others and assume the world is filled with meanness. In fact, we think the world is a terrible place. We moan and groan. We eventually lose our family, our friends. We become sorry sights and we don't even know why. Worse, the disease we have is infectious. Innocent people we encounter are susceptible to catching fear and dread from us, including our children. We know something's wrong, but we don't know how to be cured.

One way to rid yourself of this infection is to stand up straight and take on the Coalwood attitude of being proud of who you are. But to be proud of who you are, it is necessary also to *know* who you are. The best way to do that is by learning the history of your family and the history of where you live. Growing up in Coalwood, my friends and I knew exactly who we were because we knew who our parents were. That might be a good place for you to start, too.

My parents were not perfect, but they were probably the most interesting people I ever knew. My father, Homer Hickam Sr., rose to the position of Coalwood's mine superintendent from the ranks of the common miner. He loved his job, and he loved Coalwood. My mother, Elsie Hickam, was an adventurous woman who had, to her way of thinking, sacrificed her own future for the man she loved. My parents, because of their different outlooks on life, sometimes argued, occasionally bitterly, but my older brother Jim and I knew they loved us and each other because we knew who they were. That knowledge made us unafraid.

When I went to the Coalwood school in the first grade, it wasn't with strangers. I grew up with all of the children in my grade, knew them practically from the day I was born. I knew all their names, knew who their parents were, knew nearly everything about them. Jimmie Carroll, Roy Lee Cooke, Sherman Siers, Benny Brown, Jimmy Evans, Linda DeHaven, Margie Jones, Billy Rose, Linda Bukovich, Peggy Hatmaker, Kiki Castellano, Alvin Stanley, Roger Lester, Connie Williams and dozens of others of us squeezed into our little desks, bright-eyed and ready to learn. We knew we were one people because of the common stories we had been told by our parents and by the other adults around us. As our teachers rose to instruct us, they knew they had students with something vastly important in common. We knew who we were, the children of brave coal miners, the children of brave mothers who were even then struggling to keep their houses clean and their households together. Our parents were also the children of the brave men and women who had built our town.

Although he died before I was born, the people of

Coalwood made certain that I and all my classmates knew as much as we could about a man by the name of Mr. George Lafayette Carter. He was the man who founded Coalwood and its sister town of Caretta, just across a mountain from us. When folks talked about Mr. Carter, they turned downright reverential in their tone as if he was as important as Moses, or George Washington or Abraham Lincoln. To Coalwood, I guess he was.

Mr. Carter was born in Carroll County, Virginia, in 1857. He was the son of a Confederate Army officer who lost a leg in the war people in Virginia liked to call the War Between the States. People in West Virginia, who had to separate from Virginia so they could stay in the Union, mostly called it "that damned war." Six foot, four inches tall, it was said Mr. Carter dominated a room just by walking into it. He was a bit of a gambler, not in games of chance, but in enterprise. By the time he was thirty years old, he had gone deeply into debt several times so as to build iron furnaces, coke ovens and a small railroad in his native Carroll County. To stoke his furnaces and ovens and fully utilize his railroad, Mr. Carter figured he needed coal—and a lot of it. He accordingly cast his eyes north, to the great awful wilderness across the border in McDowell County in the new state of West Virginia. Others had also seen the promise of this wild country but warned Mr. Carter against it. Death and worse (losing money) awaited any and all who dared try to build anything in that inhospitable land.

Undaunted by those with lesser courage, Mr. Carter found himself a good mule and, in 1887, headed north to where there were no roads, only narrow, overgrown paths left by the old Cherokee hunting parties and meandering herds of deer. After traveling for several days, Mr. Carter came upon a narrow little valley where, to his astonishment, he beheld a thick layer of shiny black coal five feet thick, eroded from a mountain bank. If such a treasure was on the surface, what a vast ocean of black diamonds must lay below! Mr. Carter went home and put together a plan. After acquiring the land from its absentee owners, he brought in workers from Carroll County and set them to digging. Day after day after week after month, his men dug through ancient layers of strata without any certainty that they would ever find anything below. The great vaulted sides of the shaft loomed over them until, at last, there was nothing but a little star-twinkle of light, and then even that was gone. But still they dug. Mr. Carter's money coffers began to feel the pinch, and soon he was back in debt. He persevered. "Keep digging, boys," he was reputed to have said. "I smell money below." Seven hundred feet straight down, his nose was proved correct. The darkest, richest, softest, metallurgical bituminous coal the world would ever know had been breeched. All that remained was to mine it out, all several billions of tons of it. For that, he needed miners. The word was sent out, not only to the surrounding states but to the world. Come to southern West Virginia, men, and there you will find work.

Work—and glory. For the kind of men who answered Mr. Carter's call quickly came to understand that not only was a new town being built but a new society, and what could be ever more glorious than being part of something so noble? It is work and glory, combined with freedom, that always builds up something great and wonderful. Just as it was the opportunity for work and glory that built Coalwood, I am convinced that the exact same things will ultimately lead humankind to the stars. But Mr. Carter was not going across the solar system. He was building a town. Men and women came from everywhere, from Pennsylvania and Kentucky and Virginia and Ohio, from all over the United States. Then Italians came, followed by Poles, Hungarians, Latvians, Russians, and Welsh and Irish and Englishmen, too. Even a Mexican family or two. They settled in and began to build their lives in Mr. Carter's new town, which he named Coalwood.

When he decided to sink another shaft across the mountain, Mr. Carter built a second town on the same template as the first and called it Caretta, a name formed by the combination of Carter and Etta, the name of Mr. Carter's fine and patrician wife. Other venture capitalists also poured into McDowell County at the same time. Soon, the towns of Kimball, Keystone, Welch, Bishop, Northfork, Elkhorn, English, Davy and dozens of others appeared, all constructed to house the miners digging into the vast layers of high-grade coal generally called the Pocahontas seam.

But none of the other towns in the county except Coalwood and Caretta had what was known as the Coalwood Proposition. It was that proposition that made the people there uniquely into one people, one grown together from many. The Coalwood Proposition was simple: If a man would come and work in his mine, Mr. Carter promised a good job with good pay, a fine house with indoor plumbing, a company store system that wouldn't price gouge, fences to keep the cows and pigs in their proper places, free medical and dental care, and excellent schools so that, in Mr. Carter's words, "Any of our children might aspire to greatness."

The Coalwood Proposition was enhanced by the arrival of a great Stanford University–trained engineer named William Laird who had served as a captain in the trenches with Mr. Carter's son. "Captain" Laird, as everybody in town called him, set about adding to the proposition by making Mr. Carter's coal mine as safe as it could possibly be. He established rules inside the mine that had to be followed, provided the equipment that would keep them safe, and even hired a man whose only job was to watch over the safety rules and regulations and make certain they were followed. Captain Laird established one of the first mine rescue teams in the country. And while he was being safe, he set his men to dig out the coal. Those men were confident that they were being led by great men. It was something that I understood at a very early age, that to be led by great men is to be great yourself.

Of course, all was not smooth and perfect during Coalwood's formative years. Mistakes were made, and even with the best of intentions, bad things were done, often by good people. Coalwood divided itself into sections: New Camp, Substation, Main Street, Snakeroot, Mudhole, Middletown and Frog Level. Snakeroot and Mudhole were for Coalwood's "colored" citizens who were respected, even loved, but kept decidedly separate. The men who worked in the mine worked side by side and emerged from their daily toil all the same color, the same shiny black of our bituminous coal. They were friends at work, but still they lived apart, and their children went to separate schools. It was a shameful fact. Eventually, those wrongs would be made right, just as in the rest of our country, but it would take awhile, and even a day was too long.

Mr. Carter also overplayed his hand from time to time, especially when it came to keeping the mining union out of our town. He believed his benevolence with his workers through the Coalwood Proposition was enough and no union was needed. But everybody, whether they were black or white, union or anti-union, respected Mr. Carter for what he had done: From nothing he had built a fine town and made it into a proud, clean and decent place to live and work.

Eventually the United Mine Workers under John L. Lewis insisted that Mr. Carter's mine be unionized. Such was the resulting turmoil, that President Harry S. Truman sent in the United States Navy, of all people, to occupy the town. Mr. Carter was long dead by then. His son, James Carter, sold out and another era began, that of ownership of Coalwood by the Olga Coal Company. During most of my growing-up years, it was that company I knew, the one my mom scornfully called "Miss Olga," which competed so completely for the affections of my father.

Coalwood was a good place with an imperfect history, and that's what we learned from our parents and in school. My parents, and the parents of my friends, and my teachers made certain I knew Coalwood history, all of it, the good and the bad, and that I understood it. Since I listened to all sides, I became proud of how Coalwood was built and proud of the people who came to be there. That made me proud to be who I was. I was one with history, one with my roots, one with the people who were always around me. There is no strength quite so great as knowing you are of one people, and that it is a good people of courage and dignity, even when they are sometimes wrong. Such knowledge gave the children of Coalwood a quiet pride, both in themselves and

all who came before them. We were never alone and therefore forever brave.

> *We know our history.*
> *We are proud of who we are.*
> *We are not afraid.*

WE ARE DOERS, NOT DREAMERS

The story of Coalwood's Rocket Boys is a good example of
fighting off fear and keeping dread at bay. I detailed their
story in my books *Rocket Boys* (also known as *October Sky*)
and *The Coalwood Way.* It is a true story of how a group of
teenage boys (five from Coalwood and one from the nearby
mining town of Bartley) came to build sophisticated rockets
that flew miles into the sky. Along the way, they won a gold
and silver medal at the 1960 National Science Fair, which
brought great honor to their parents, their teachers, themselves and the little towns from which they came. It is a tale
of the triumph of dreams coming true. I could write down
their story pretty easily since I was the leader of the group
that came to be known as the Rocket Boys.

Quite often when I'm on book tour, a parent will present
herself to me at the signing table and ask that I inscribe one
of my books to her child. "Tell him to keep dreaming," she'll
proudly say. I usually do as the parent asks but what I'd really
like to do is to suggest that what I learned as a Rocket Boy
was that dreaming never amounts to much. It's the *doing*
that counts. In fact, I believe dreaming and not doing is just
another manifestation of the habit of being afraid.

As an example, perhaps a young woman wants to be a NASCAR auto mechanic. Her parents take her to the races, and there she dreams of what it would be like to be down in the pits as part of a skilled team. She watches races on television, all the while imagining that she could be one of those talented mechanics. She tells her parents and teachers that she wants to be a NASCAR auto mechanic, and she is patted on the head for it. She is made to feel special because she has such a grand dream, but neither her parents or her teachers suggest that if she's got a dream, she'd better get busy making it come true. Instead, she is allowed to just dream, and before she knows it, she's twenty-something years old and she's never gotten started, doesn't know a spanner wrench from a pneumatic jack. It's too late for her dream, although it remained perfectly intact during all those years. For a reason even she can't quite define, she never did anything to realize it. But the reason is simple. She and her parents and teachers had bought into the notion that dreaming is enough. It never is.

I am often asked how it felt to finally reach my boyhood dream of working for NASA. I can tell you my career with the space agency was a very satisfying one. I'm glad my dream turned into reality, but it didn't just happen because I dreamed it. I had to work like the devil to make it come true, beginning with the building and launching of my rockets in Coalwood.

It was a great shock to the United States when the Russians launched *Sputnik,* the world's first man-made satellite, in October 1957. The newspapers we received in Coalwood were filled with stories of how American scientists and engineers were desperately working to catch up in the space race, especially a man named Dr. Wernher von Braun. Dr. von Braun became my instant hero. It was as if the science fiction I had read all my life was coming true. I started to think about what an adventure it would be to work for Dr. von Braun. For all I knew, a man with that much conviction might even form an expedition into space, like Lewis and Clark. I wanted to be part of that team. To be eligible to join up, I knew I would have to prepare myself in some way, get some special knowledge about something. I was kind of vague on what it would be, but I could at least see I would need to be like the heroes in my science fiction books, brave and knowing more than the next man.

I gathered together five other boys, and we formed a club we called the Big Creek Missile Agency (BCMA). Quentin Wilson (a boy from Bartley) was the brains of the outfit. O'Dell Carroll was the scrounger. Roy Lee Cooke was the lovemaster (you'll have to read the books to find out why), Billy Rose was the tracker, and Sherman Siers was our propellant-mixer. My job was to lead the group and to figure out what to do next when things didn't work out. When we began, we didn't know what we were doing, but after some initial disasters, the people of Coalwood, especially my mother and our teachers started to rally around us to see how they could help. The preacher at the church convinced the coal company officials (specifically my father) to let us use an old slack dump just outside of town as our rocket range, and several master machinists volunteered their time and skill to help us build our designs. At our high school, a very special science teacher, Miss Freida Riley, got us a book on rocketry that required us to learn advanced mathematics. She gave it to us with a challenge: "All I've done is give you a book," she said. "You have to have to courage to learn what's inside it." We learned, we built, we tested and we improved our designs until we were flying rockets miles into the sky.

Eventually, the BCMA won a medal at the National Science Fair. We were proud of what we had done, but the credit really went to the people of Coalwood. Without their support, we would have never been able to build our rockets. We had started as dreamers but we had turned into doers, and that was the important lesson of the Rocket Boys. It was a lesson I never forgot. I even applied it to my career as a writer. After years of struggling to get published, I wrote a book called *Torpedo Junction*, a book about the battle against the U-boats along the American East Coast during World War II. I worked for years on it, even diving to the deep wrecks off Cape Hatteras to research exactly what had happened. Even with all the work I did, the book was only a moderate success. Still, I'd been published. It was a start. I kept going. I wrote even while I was working for NASA on some difficult projects that made me keep long hours. To compensate, I got up very early and wrote before I went to work. When I came home, no matter how late it was, I'd write until I couldn't keep my eyes open. I wrote every weekend. I kept trying. My next book turned out to be *Rocket Boys*. It became a #1 *New York Times* bestseller, and Universal Studios made it into the movie *October Sky*. I had dreamed, but I had also done while not being afraid of failure.

Here are a few simple concepts about how to turn your dreams into reality. First, you should have a real passion for whatever you dream because to make it come true, you've got to be willing to work harder than anybody else. Then, once you're committed to doing the work, you have to get a plan. Without planning and an organized approach to whatever it is you want to do, you are going nowhere. That means figuring out all the steps it takes to reach a goal. What education is required? How does one apply for the position? What attributes are most likely to get you into that position? Study others who have done something similar to what you want to do. Model yourself after them as much as possible. Then go after your dream by following your plan. But there's one thing more. Neither passion nor planning will get you where you want to go without perseverance. Perseverance means never giving up. You must keep plugging away, no matter what obstacles crop up along the way. These are what I call the three Ps of success: passion, planning and perseverance. It is the doing, not the dreaming that counts. That's what I learned as a Coalwood Rocket Boy.

Not everything I have attempted has worked over the years. We all fail, being humans, but that is part of the glory of success. In fact, I believe the steps taken to reach a dream often are the best part of the journey. To dream, to wish, to hope, all those are good and worthy emotions but they're not worth anything without the willingness to sweat a little. Another lesson of the Rocket Boys is it isn't always the most intelligent who reach their dreams. Successful people are the ones willing to roll up their sleeves and work hard. It's one of those axioms of life that must be recognized. As O'Dell used to say, a rocket won't fly unless somebody lights the fuse. To reach your dreams, take that first step, then the next and then the next. Then keep going. You'll get there.

We are doers, not dreamers.
We are proud of who we are.
We are not afraid.

WE HAVE IMPORTANT JOBS TO DO

I am convinced that one of the greatest sources of courage and strength is to have an important job to do. My boyhood observation of Coalwood people was that they all knew what their jobs were and were convinced of their importance. I believe this attitude about what they did for a living was one of the things that made them fundamentally unafraid. What motivated my father and the other miners in Coalwood's deep and dangerous mine was not always clear to me. Most of the time while I was growing up, I thought they were just doing their jobs, even though I couldn't help but notice that they seemed inordinately proud of what they did. It was only after I grew up and left that I began to understand that so many people in this world have jobs that they dislike and believe to be unimportant. I also began to realize how debilitating that can be to the spirit. My dad and his men went to work with good cheer even though every day they went into a place that could easily kill them. Yet they were proud and willing because they were convinced that what they were doing was bigger, and therefore more glorious, than themselves.

A section in the mine called 11 East is a good example of this approach to work. The job that was done there became a legend in Coalwood. I knew the story as well as anybody, having heard it from my parents at the supper table many times. It was Captain Laird who first opened 11 East. It was early

1941, war clouds were looming, and it was certain the United States would need lots of steel. To make the best steel, a very pure grade of coal was required, and Coalwood's coal was the best metallurgical coal there was. The Captain, however, wanted an even purer coal. Core samples had showed him where there was a huge seam of extremely low-sulfur bituminous coal. It was believed to be seven to nine feet thick, easy-to-work "high coal" as such was called. The only problem was a huge rock header—a massive slab of rock—that stood between the men of Coalwood and this vast reservoir of coal. Undaunted, the Captain pointed a crew at it. Despite the Captain's confidence, it didn't take long before 11 East turned into Coalwood's nightmare. There were rock falls, runaway cars, gas flare-ups, flooding, and some men were hurt and a few were killed.

Dad was a day-shift construction foreman at the time when 11 East was opened, but the Captain reassigned him to take the lead foreman's job on the evening shift of the new section. Day after day, the Coalwood men on all three shifts assaulted 11 East like an army at war, trying every way possible to get through the bad rock. Then, to compound their problems, they discovered that the new seam sloped downward and became narrower. Before it was over, men had to crawl on their hands and knees to get to the face, but the Captain kept urging them on. Only the Japanese attack on Pearl Harbor stopped the combat at 11 East. With the demand for coal from the War Department, the Captain had no choice but to assign his men to other working parts of the mine.

My dad never forgot 11 East, and neither did the Captain, but circumstances kept them from going after it for many years. When the Captain retired in 1954, my father took over the job of mine superintendent. Four years later, when the demand of coal increased enough to warrant getting permission to proceed from the owners, my dad went after 11 East again, determined to do the job this time no matter what it took. For weeks, he kept his men at it, drilling through solid rock. He brought in advisors from Germany to put in a new kind of mining equipment, giant machines called long-wall cutters. Then, one snowy night, in a last-ditch assault, the men of Coalwood finally punched through the rock and found the coal, a tall seam of the richest, darkest, lowest-sulfur coal anybody had ever imagined could exist, just as the Captain said it would. I wrote about that miracle, and other miracles, in *The Coalwood Way.*

Although the victory over 11 East was certainly a wonderful thing, beating something formidable was not the lesson to be drawn from it. It is an easy thing to say the men of Coalwood were brave, which they were, or that they felt a sense of duty, which they did, or that they were stubbornly opposed to losing, which nobody ever doubted. But what else? The lesson to be drawn is that they were successful because they saw the importance of a job bigger than themselves.

I had an inkling of how important his job was to him when my father first took me into the mine. I was fifteen years old at the time. Dad had come to the opinion that perhaps I could do for him what he had done for the Captain, and that was prepare myself to take over from him the important job of Coalwood's mine superintendent. Dad also desperately wanted me to become a mining engineer and gain a college diploma, something he did not have.

After Dad had shown me the choreography of the machinery and the men at the working face, we headed outside. As we trundled back down the main line aboard a man-trip, I was thinking about all that I had seen. Then my father, a man who shared very few words with me during my entire life, suddenly started to talk. "I love the mine," he said. "I love everything about it. I love getting up in the morning before sunrise and walking up the path to the tipple. I love seeing the shifts change, the men bunching up at the man-hoist, ready to go to work."

I listened, amazed, not that he was saying what he was saying, but that he would share such thoughts with me. I felt proud and grown-up. Dad took off his helmet and rubbed his head, scratching around it where the sides of the helmet had pressed in his hair. When he started to talk again, I focused on his every word. "I love going to the face. I go every day even though I don't have to. That's where I see if my plan for the day is working. I see it all in my head days before, see the cut the continuous mining machines will take, the route of the loaders, the roof bolts going in, the places where the methane might build up and where the foreman needs to check with his safety lamp. It's all there when I arrive, just as I saw it, and I get great satisfaction from that.

"Every day," he said, "I meet with my boss and the engineers. Even though I don't have a college diploma, I know more than they do because I've been to the face and they haven't. I've ridden the man-trip down the main line, got out and walked back into the gob and felt the air pressure on my face. I know the mine like I know a man; I can sense things about it that aren't right even when everything on paper says

it is. Every day there's something that needs to be done—
because men will be hurt if it isn't done, or the coal the company's promised to load won't get loaded. Coal is the
lifeblood of this country. If we fail, steel fails, and then the
country fails."
      The beam from his helmet lamp shone in my eyes.
"There's no men in the world like miners, Sonny. They're
good men, strong men. The best there is. I think no matter
what you do with your life, no matter where you go or who
you know, you will never know such good and strong men.
      "You're my boy," he said and then turned so his lamp
shined down a side cut, the lamps of his men flashing back
from the darkness as if they knew he was passing. "I was
born to lead men in the profession of mining coal. Maybe
you were, too."
      In the dark, I could savor my father's words without
embarrassment. But that was all I could do. I had to disap-
point my father that day by telling him I couldn't be what he
wanted me to be. I had other dreams. I wanted to be an
aerospace engineer and build rockets and help America go
into space. But I never forgot what Dad said about the mine
and miners. And when I tried to figure out why it was he and
his men lived a life without fear, I realized he'd told me a
very important part of it.
      When I was writing *Sky of Stone,* the third memoir in the
Coalwood trilogy, I dug into a box of my father's papers looking
for something that would tell me what kind of leader he was to
his men. To my astonishment, I found a document, a yellowing
sheet of paper, where he'd written the attributes of a mine foreman. This was the basis for the lecture he gave his new foremen
on their responsibilities to the company and to the men who

would rely on them to be fair and good supervisors. Here is that list:

The Attributes of an Olga Foreman

- We are proud of who we are. We were chosen to be Olga men.
- We are morally straight. We don't lie, cheat, steal or keep around those who do. That not only goes for work, but everywhere.
- We never stop learning.
- We give orders and take orders like a man.
- We don't make deals. We tell our men what to do and then stick to it.
- We don't watch the clock. We get to work early and leave only when the job is finished.
- We don't make decisions on what somebody else said. We go and see things for ourselves.
- When things go wrong, we don't hunt for someone else to blame. We fix it.
- We don't buddy with our crews.
- We're not afraid to tell a man he's no good. A man can't get good if he doesn't know he's bad.
- We're the boss. We never tell the men to do something because somebody else said so. We say so, and we make sure they do it.
- We know production is the key. Without it, all the good things we have in Coalwood and Caretta, our homes, our schools and all that we hold dear, all will be lost.

Dad's list is an excellent management document. Any

manager in any business would be wise to learn it and use it. They will not fail if they follow it. But the list reflects more than just solid management principles. This list showed the way my father thought about what he did and what his foremen did. They believed the work they did in the mine was a thing greater than themselves. Note that my dad wrote that not only should they be moral and upright at work, but at home, too. They were company men, twenty-four hours a day, every day, and that gave them a special responsibility. They were proud of who they were because they believed that what they did was important and a thing bigger than themselves. It was not only important to themselves, their families, the company and the town, but to their country and the world. They dug the coal from which steel was made, and steel, in their opinion, was the structure on which the very foundation of civilization rested.

Being fulfilled in one's work washes away much of the fear of living, and it should be your goal to find that work. If you're young and just starting out, the road is wide open for you to find work that is satisfying and important. If you're older and seem stuck in an occupation, especially if you have a family to support and can't easily walk away from an income, you should still seek to escape the fear and unhappiness that a meaningless job can cause. One thing you can do is change the way you think about what you do. If you are doing a job, by its very definition, it is necessary. When you're doing it, don't hold back. Give it everything you've got. Make what you do, no matter how trivial or unimportant you think it is, special to yourself. Search for things about it that are good and giving to the community. Stay longer at it, give your boss a little extra (even if you don't like him or her), and search for anything that will give your job new and special meaning. And never forget that if your job allows you to feed and clothe your family and yourself, then you are engaged in a job bigger than yourself. If you change the way you think about what you do, you'll be like the people of Coalwood and be able to say:

> *We have important jobs to do.*
> *We are proud of who we are.*
> *We are not afraid.*

WE BRING HONOR TO OUR PEOPLE

To be proud of who you are, you should bring honor to your people. Plutarch wrote that it is a desirable thing to be well descended, but the glory belongs to your ancestors. In other words, it isn't enough to take credit for things that were done by others, even if those others were your parents and relatives. It is necessary that you do things that add to the honor and glory of your people and where you live, or go to school or work. If you do these things, you will be proud of yourself and unafraid because you will have proved that you are deserving to belong to those around you.

When I was a boy, I observed that the adults in Coalwood did everything they could to teach us that we had a responsibility to add to the town's glory. Sports was one way to do that, and our football and basketball games at the Coalwood School were considered vitally important. Winning, it was often remarked, was good for everybody, not just the winner. Every game was attended by everyone who could go, and the cheers for every player, even the ones who only occasionally got off the bench, were almost enough to be heard down in the coal mine. A Coalwood team could also win even if it came up short on the number of points on the scoreboard. It could win if it played its heart out, too. Coal miners and their wives could tell if one of their teams was playing with all the guts and sweat they had. If they did that, then they won and make no mistake.

There was another way to bring honor and glory to Coalwood that had nothing to do with sports. It was to make good grades in school. Report cards of every child were shared up and down the gossip fence-line. To bring home good grades was every bit as wonderful as scoring a touchdown in a football game. Academic reports, when they came out, were a topic of conversation in our homes, in our churches and in our company stores. We children knew very well that if we had made good grades, we had brought honor to everybody. If we hadn't done as well as we could, then we were encouraged to try harder, not just for ourselves but for everyone in town so they could be proud of us. There was also an ultimate educational glory. It was called the Golden Horseshoe.

The Golden Horseshoe was the award given to the top four eighth-grade students in each county in an annual West Virginia history competition. Winners traveled to the capital city of Charleston to appear before the governor, who would touch their shoulders with a big sword and proclaim them Knights of the Golden Horseshoe. The best history students in the Coalwood School were selected every year to go after a Golden Horseshoe, and nearly every year, one of those children won one for the town. It was a source of great pride. People would spy the winning child and ask to see the prize, which was only a little golden pin, but it would be held out with great ceremony and gazed at with rapt admiration. Although I knew how important it was, a Golden Horseshoe was nothing I ever imagined that I might win. In fact, taking a test in history or anything else was nothing I ever did very well. My West Virginia history teacher in the eighth grade was Mrs. Virginia Mahoney, the wife of "Spud" Mahoney, an outside mine foreman. Mrs. Mahoney was also my arithmetic teacher. She was a serious woman with a voice that seemed to carry with it an ancient wisdom. Whether she was teaching long division or how our state became the unlucky site of the first land battle of the Civil War, Mrs. Mahoney carried with her a dignity and a seriousness of purpose that made me pay attention, at least as much as my often-wandering brain would allow.

This might be a good place to explain something. My father was Homer Hickam Sr. I am Homer Hickam Jr., even though I was the second son. The story goes that the first time my dad ever saw me, he said, "That's the ugliest baby I've ever seen!" and turned and walked out of Mom's hospital room. The next person in was a nurse with a clipboard. "And what are we naming this little baby boy?" she asked, officiously. My mother snarled, "I think we're going to name this one after his father." Homer turned out to be too big of a name for me, so it didn't take long before I acquired the nickname Sonny. And Sonny was what I was called the entire time I was growing up in Coalwood. When somebody calls me Sonny now, it's always someone who knew me as a boy.

No matter what my name was, the truth is I simply was never a good student. The problem was I liked to daydream, and I liked to do just about anything other than study or work hard in class. I once wrapped my arithmetic book cover around *The Black Stallion* when I was supposed to be puzzling my way through some arithmetic problems in Mrs. Mahoney's class. When she caught me, inevitable now that I think about it, she took me out into the hall and proceeded to question me closely. Her questions were put forward in a hushed voice. My answers were equally hushed. We both had to speak low, lest we attract the attention of Mr. Likens, the school principal, who would probably insist on doling out some appropriate punishment for a student so sorry as to have to be taken to the hall. Speaking as softly as I knew how, I confessed reading *The Black Stallion* was far more fun than doing arithmetic.

"Do you believe, then," Mrs. Mahoney asked, "that this is the purpose of coming to school, so that you might have fun?"

"Well," I answered, "if it isn't too much trouble, I wouldn't mind having some fun here."

Mrs. Mahoney considered my answer. "You are an interesting child," she allowed, and then said, "I believe I know how you might have fun and still proceed with your studies. You, Sonny Hickam, will be one of our students to take the Golden Horseshoe test this year!"

I was astonished, but not so much I didn't immediately try to squirm my way out of it. "I am sorry for any fun I might have ever had here, and I will do my best to not ever have any again," I said, forgetting to hush my voice. "And I sure don't want to take that test!"

Mrs. Mahoney allowed a twinkle in her eye and then got back to business. "I'm serious about this, Sonny," she said.

Then she looked over her shoulder, and we both saw that Mr. Likens was coming. The backside of my pants suddenly felt entirely too thin. Mr. Likens had a paddle with holes in it, reserved for serious miscreants. Mr. Likens took in the scene and asked what the trouble was. While I gulped, Mrs. Mahoney said, "Sonny is going to take the Golden Horseshoe test, Mr. Likens. It's a fun thing to do, and he likes to have fun, don't you, dear?"

To protect my nether regions from Mr. Likens's paddle, I supposed it would be fun and said so out loud, and there it was. I was going to have to do it. It didn't take me two seconds before I was there in my imagination, kneeling before the governor on a purple pillow, my chin up, my shoulders squared and the great flat sword coming down to touch me once, twice—

"Sonny," Mrs. Mahoney sighed, seeing that I'd gone off into a reverie, "if you have any chance of winning, you're going to have to study and study hard!"

It was all a big challenge, that much was for sure. When I got home, I told my mother of Mrs. Mahoney's decision. "I'm going to win the Golden Horseshoe," I told her with a confidence I didn't feel.

Mom was perched on a stepladder working on a big mural she was painting on our kitchen wall. It was a mural of Myrtle Beach, South Carolina, the faraway place where she hoped someday to live. She stopped for a moment, her brush held in mid air, and replied, "I think I should like to see you win, Sonny." And then she went back to making her swipes at the mural which, at the time, was just getting started. All she had was a bit of a beach, a little sky and not much of the ocean at all. Eventually, some years later, it would be a grand painting of a wonderful, sunny landscape. She was getting to it, little by little. Some people said she was painting herself into a different reality where her husband didn't go to work every day in a dangerous mine and where her second son didn't go around fooling himself that he might be smart enough to win something so grand and difficult as the Golden Horseshoe test.

In my room, I kept thinking about the Golden Horseshoe. Then, recalling Mrs. Mahoney's advice that I had to work hard, I took out my West Virginia history book and began to read. Soon, I was lost inside it, tramping with ol' Daniel Boone as he passed through our land on his way to Kentucky, with the first pioneers trying to grub out a living on our rocky hillsides, with the soldiers fighting through our tangled woods in Civil War battles, and with our Chuck Yeager as he climbed inside his rocket plane, the X-1, and made history by being the first person to break the sound barrier. Pretty soon, I was having fun. I guess I got to whooshing around the room with Chuck Yeager because I scared my cat, Daisy Mae, who ran off with an offended mew. But I kept studying, in my own dramatic fashion. After awhile, it was almost even fun.

As usual, it didn't take me too long to get carried away at what I was doing. I studied every day and every night. I studied when my friends were out sledding in the snow, and I studied when they were playing hide-and-go-seek amongst the spring flowers. I went to the Coalwood School library and checked out everything about West Virginia I could find. Mrs. Mahoney arranged for me to be drilled by volunteer tutors from the ninth grade, including Eleanor Marie Dantzler, the daughter of the company store manager, who had won the Golden Horseshoe the year before. There was nobody smarter than Eleanor Marie Dantzler. She advised me to study lists, lots and lots of lists.

By then, I was really into it. I studied the lists of state hospitals and where they were located and what they did. I studied the lists of all the big state officials and the judges. I studied the lists of all the counties and learned their names and the names of their county seats. I learned the state animal (black bear) and the state bird (cardinal) and the state tree (sugar maple). I amused and abused my friends by demanding that they ask me questions about West Virginia, anything at all. I tried to get them to stump me and when they did, I learned the answer and was a better, smarter boy for it.

After awhile, I began to bask in my coming glory. People on the street, the miners going to and from the mine, the women going in and out of the company stores, the preacher at the churches, all wanted to know how I was doing with my studies. When I told my best adult friend in town, the Reverend Richard, that I was going to win the Golden Horseshoe, he sat me down on the steps in front of the little church that had been built for the black folks in town. The Reverend called it the Mudhole Church of Distinct Christianity. "I pray that you win, Sonny," he said. "But the Lord don't always give us what we want when we want it. Some things take time."

I couldn't imagine what the Reverend meant, although I didn't say so. I thanked him and asked him to ask me a question on West Virginia, got one, answered it, and went on my way. I was certain I was ready and that I was going to win.

At last the grand day came. I went to the school all dressed up in my Sunday school best. Mrs. Mahoney was to take me

to Welch High School, which was located across the mountain in the county seat, where the test would be given. But
when I presented myself to her classroom, I was told she was
ill. Coach Tom Morgan, Coalwood's football coach, would be
taking me to Welch.

I liked Coach Morgan. He was a fine fellow, a born-and-
bred and grown-up Coalwood boy himself. He had just
recently come back from a combat tour in Korea. I was
proud to get to ride to Welch in his car, even though I would
miss last-minute tutoring by Mrs. Mahoney.

At Welch High School, the test was given out. It was a
thick one, a booklet of questions. On the back was a map of
the state. The first question was to put in all the state hospitals and county seats. I could do that so I did it right off.
Then I took the rest of the test. There were a few stumpers.
I wasn't sure about several of the questions, but I made good
guesses. I figured I got most of them.

Afterwards, I sat outside in the hall and waited for the
results. I wasn't alone. Students from all over the county
were there, sitting on benches lined up and down along the
walls. We eyed one another, strangers but somehow brothers
and sisters, too. We had all taken the great test. It was
enough to bind us together. We sneaked looks at one
another. I even talked to a few of them. I felt very grown-up
to know kids who didn't live in Coalwood and Caretta.

An hour passed. Then another. It got dark outside. What
was taking so long? At last, the doors burst open and the
teachers came out and went to their children to tell the
results. Shouts of joy rang out along with moans of disappointment. Coach Morgan came up to me and I rose from
my chair. "You didn't win," he said quickly. "But you lost by

only one point and that point was in dispute. I argued for you. That's what took us so long. But I finally got overruled. I'm sorry, Sonny."

Sudden despair welled up inside me. *I had lost.* I couldn't imagine it. But there was no denying it. There was only one chance in the entire history of my life to ever win a Golden Horseshoe, and I had failed. My life, such as it was, was over. No matter what might happen to me in the future, no matter what else I might attain, I would not win the Golden Horseshoe. I was a miserable failure. I sort of more or less hoped that the world would end. To my disappointment, it kept turning right along.

Mrs. Mahoney was the first one to tell me I hadn't failed, not exactly. "I could have gotten you that point, Sonny," she said. "Coach Morgan is a good man, but he didn't know how to fight those old teachers in Welch. I would have worn them down for you. They just figured they'd show a young teacher they were in charge, and that's why they wouldn't let Coach get you your point no matter how hard he tried. Now, stop moping around and hold your head up. You learned a lot in trying, and I'm not the least bit sorry that I had you take the test for us. You didn't do your best. If you had, you would have won. But you learned that you can learn, and I guess we have to be satisfied with that. Now, go do something else for Coalwood."

Mrs. Mahoney was right, although it took me a while to believe it. Four years later, I went off to the National Science Fair and won a medal, bringing great honor to our town. I figured it was the least I could do, considering how I'd failed to win the Golden Horseshoe.

It would be many years later, over forty in fact, before I

again recalled my first failed chance to win glory for Coalwood. I found myself standing in front of none other than Governor Cecil Underwood, the governor of West Virginia. Cecil Underwood had been elected governor the same year I'd taken the Golden Horseshoe test. He was West Virginia's youngest governor and later became its oldest, too. "Homer," he said, "with your books and the movie, you have brought great honor to the state of West Virginia. What can we do for you?"

I couldn't help myself. I blurted, "I want my Golden Horseshoe!" It just popped out of me.

Startled, the governor stared for a moment, then laughed out loud. After answering a few questions on a pop quiz, I got my Golden Horseshoe. Mrs. Mahoney, Coach Morgan, my parents and all the people in Coalwood were finally being honored for believing in me. That little pin was as much theirs as it was mine. To keep honoring them, I wear it nearly all the time in public.

One other thing, too. The Reverend Richard was right. The Lord doesn't always give us what we want when we want it. Some things just take a little time.

We bring honor to our people.
We are proud of who we are.
We are not afraid.

WE DON'T QUIT

One of the greatest lessons I received in Coalwood was that once you started a thing, you didn't give up on it. You could change what you were doing to meet unexpected situations but you kept going, no matter what, until you reached your goal. Some people these days call that kind of attitude hard-headed, stubborn and even foolish. Coalwood folks sometimes called it those things, too, but they always admired it anyway. They knew quitting is one of the best ways to tear down your self-respect and therefore should be avoided at all costs. Coalwood people thought quitting was far worse than failure. Failure, they said, was only temporary. Quitting is always permanent. It's also another way of being afraid.

Every day, my father's foremen gathered in his office to get their orders. Sometimes, when I had a day off from school, I'd sneak up to the tipple to watch and listen. It always made me proud the way Dad controlled the interest of these big, tough coal miners. They hung on his every word. Dad went over the situation in each of the sections of the mine, detailing problems, making suggestions and telling each man what was expected in terms of production. His foremen listened, asked a few questions and then went to work, determined to reach the goals my father had set. I heard a new foreman one time wonder aloud what he should do if the continuous miner on his section broke down. (A continuous miner was a big machine on tracks with a long boom on the end of it with rotating teeth that tore coal away from the seam.) "Should I just wait until somebody comes to fix it?" he wondered.

Before Dad could answer, one of his foremen did it for him. "We don't quit for nothing," he said. "If the machines don't work, get your men some shovels and start shoveling. You shovel with them, too."

All the foremen grinned at one another as Dad benevolently

smiled. *We don't quit for nothing.* He'd taught them well. It might have been a double negative that my English teachers would have corrected, but its meaning was loud and clear. We have an important job to do and we don't quit doing it in this mine, no matter what obstacles pop up in front of us.

On their sections, the foremen gave their orders and their men, all seasoned miners, heard them out, asked questions and then turned to their jobs. When I later worked in the mine during the summers while I went to college, I saw that Coalwood miners were smart and tenacious, a brilliant combination. And they didn't stop, no matter what. They might run into a dozen or more problems each day—bad roof, flooding, methane or breakdown of their equipment—but they still kept going, working around and through the situation. They didn't just sit down and wait for someone else to come and solve their problems. They used their knowledge of coal mining, their initiative and their native intellect to move forward. At the end of the day, the miners emerged, their blackened faces streaked with sweat, tired but proud of what they had accomplished. They hadn't quit, and they weren't about to start. Knowing that of themselves and all who worked with them made them proud and unafraid. They stood together as one team.

Quitting is one of those things that doesn't have to be learned. You can just fall into it, let things slide, allow sloth to rule your life, take the trouble-free way out. Quitting is an easy thing to do. There's lots of company and support if you quit, especially from other quitters. There's lots of reasons to quit, too. Whatever you're trying to do might be too hard or inconvenient or just not fun anymore. It's about the easiest thing on earth to do until you find that it's developed into a habit. Then you're in trouble. I know. It was once a habit with me. Luckily, I was living in Coalwood at the time, a place that was always more than willing to cull out any weaknesses I or any other boy or girl might develop. It seemed to me, as a very young boy, that starting a thing was the most fun, but nearly everything that happened after that got progressively harder. After awhile, my mind wanted to go and do something else. In the middle of building a castle with blocks and rocks in the backyard, I'd abandon it to go get my crayons and work on some coloring books. I'd get them half-colored and throw them down and go off, maybe looking for bugs. I'd investigate a few beetles, then go on down to the creek and help my buddies Roy Lee Cooke or Benny Brown catch some crawl-dads. Before I'd caught even one, I'd be skipping rocks across the creek while the boys yelled at me to stop scaring the critters. It was a fine tactic, this never quite finishing anything. How could I be criticized if I never quite did what I set out to do?

My mother took note of my tendency for leaving things undone right off, but she was a bit benevolent toward it. "Sonny's lazy," she'd say, "but he's not much trouble." I kept loping along, cheerfully quitting most everything I did when it got boring or too hard. Then my third-grade teacher, Mrs. Laird, the Captain's wife, wrote on my report card, "Sonny doesn't always do his work on time. He starts something and then he stops before he's done and goes off and does something else."

That note hit my house like a thunderclap! It was one thing for my mother to placidly observe my tendency to not finish what I'd started but quite another for a teacher, especially Mrs. Laird, to actually write it down on a report

card. Shocked by this observation made by such an important person, Mom knew that my attitude would have to be
changed. The first thing she did was sit me down and tell
me, in no uncertain terms, that I would never quit a thing
again that I started, *ever*. Then, while I absorbed her admonition, so vast I was having trouble getting my mind around
it, she told me that quitting was the mark of failure. She
went over people she'd known who were quitters. She had
trouble coming up with one, considering that she was the
daughter and grand-daughter of coal miners, but she did her
best, recalling a few unhappy souls from down in Florida
where she'd lived for a short time. Those people (all men
now that I think about it) were always unhappy, she said.
They were unable to provide for themselves or their
families. Sometimes, they even wound up in jails. Worse,
they were a source of shame for the people who raised them.
"I will not be ashamed of one of my boys," she said. "You will
change yourself, and you will do it *right now*."

I was anxious to please her, but I wasn't certain how to do
it, at least at that very moment. For one thing, I didn't have
anything that I was doing right then, except for listening to
her lecture, which I did without quitting even once. I hoped
that would be the end of it but, of course, it wasn't. Her next
move was to pass along my shortcoming over the gossip-
fence. It didn't take long before I was well aware that my dis-
grace was town knowledge. Roy Lee, Benny and I had to
fight a rock battle with some boys out of Frog Level because
they called me a quitter to my face. It suddenly wasn't particularly easy being my friend. My buddies stuck with me,
but I could tell they sure hoped I would soon change my
ways and stop being an embarrassment. My Sunday school

teacher, Mr. Baker, even remarked on my unhappy trait, telling us the story of old Daniel who never quit what he did, even when he got thrown in the lion's den. He looked at me the whole time he told it. I had only just turned eight years old, but I was old enough to know that whenever my Sunday school teacher based his lesson on one of my shortcomings, I was in trouble, big trouble. There was only one way to get out of it. I threw myself on Mrs. Laird's mercy to somehow get her to put on my report card that I wasn't a quitter. "Write me a story, beginning to end," she said.

I'd always been a good reader, and reading had given me a natural love of writing, too. I loved to start writing stories, but I invariably lost interest and stopped before I got very far. I'd shown Mrs. Laird a couple of my partial attempts, and she'd admired them. But when she had tried to get me to finish one, I never had. She'd been disappointed and had said so, out loud. I should have listened to her. Coalwood teachers didn't say things out loud to their students just for the fun of it. It occurs to me now that maybe Mrs. Laird put her comment on my card just because she wanted me to finish one of my stories. If so, it was underhanded but certainly not beyond a Coalwood teacher who would do what she had to do to educate even the weakest of minds placed before her.

Since I had begged for mercy, I had no choice but to do what Mrs. Laird demanded of me. I would write her a story, beginning to end, and I wouldn't quit until I had done it. After giving it some thought, I decided to write about Horatio at the bridge, don't ask me why. Maybe I liked his name. I got going. I described old Horatio and wrote up a little story about the old city of Rome and how Horatio stationed himself at a bridge in the back of town to stop barbarians from getting inside. That was the easy part. But what then? How could I make this an interesting story? After I gave it some more thought, I came up with the idea that maybe Horatio knew a boy who was about my age. He was a boy who was always being accused of never finishing anything. But when the bridge was attacked, he had to slip through enemy lines to work his way to the Roman Emperor to tell him what Horatio was doing and, if the emperor didn't mind, he might send a little help. It was a hard, dangerous task, and more than once, the boy thought how much easier it would be if he just quit and went off to playing. But he didn't quit. My story ended with the boy being a big hero, of course, for finishing what he'd started.

Mrs. Laird loved the story and even mimeographed it and spread it all around the school. Soon, I had fans from even upstairs in the junior high school. Everybody wanted to know when I was going to write my next story, and hardly anybody seemed to remember that I had once been a quitter. To keep them in that frame of mind, I had to get going on my next story, and when I finished that one, I saw that I'd better write another. I was soon in great demand to keep up my stories. Mrs. Laird even said someday I would make my living as a writer. I was proud of who I was. I was a writer. But most of all, I wasn't a quitter.

Mrs. Laird wrote on my next report card, "Sonny has much improved on finishing his work."

It was faint praise but at least the pressure was off. The word of my improvement went flying across the fence until everybody in town knew about it. People in Coalwood stopped worrying about that particular flaw in my character and waited until another one surfaced so they could fix it, too.

We don't quit.
We are proud of who we are.
We are not afraid.

WE DON'T GET PUFFED UP

Coalwood adults believed that no one should ever get above himself or take on the trappings of false pride. It was a prime Coalwood sin to be proud out loud about yourself. Once, when I thought I had done something particularly intelligent and remarked on it, a company preacher took me by my arm and said, "When a man thinks himself clever, he's but a temptation to God's sense of humor." In other words, it is never wise to get too full of yourself because life has a way of properly knocking you down if you do. The pride that was taught in my town was not a boastful pride. It was a quiet pride in our culture.

One of the surest ways to lose confidence and start to be afraid is to have an exaggerated self-importance that has little or no foundation. It's a certainty that eventually you're going to be brought back to reality, and the letdown can be quite a shock. After that, it takes awhile to build yourself back up. That was one of the main reasons people in Coalwood never allowed any of their citizens to become "puffed up." Even if we built a rocket ship and flew it to the moon, the only thing allowed was to be dutifully praised. The accomplishment was then left alone to be what it was, part of the history of our town. And if the person who had done the great thing knew what was good for him, he let it alone, too.

There was once a man in Coalwood whom I will call Buddy. Buddy was the son of an old Coalwood family and known as a good man, although he was known to brag more than a little. He'd been a football hero at Big Creek High School and somehow he'd never quite outgrown the adulation that had come his way. But he was a fine worker, so fine that Dad promoted him to be a continuous miner operator, one of the most important jobs in the mine. A continuous miner was not an easy machine to operate. Someone at its controls could easily damage it by letting its teeth hit the solid rock on the roof or on the floor. A continuous mining machine was also like a tank in the constricted area where it worked. If the operator didn't watch what he was doing, he could run over the other miners who worked nearby.

Buddy took to his training well, working for some weeks as an assistant operator until it was determined that he was up to running one of the big machines by himself. He was called in to talk to Dad, who apprised him of his new assignment, continuous mining machine operator on a section during the evening shift. It was the biggest moment in Buddy's young life and, afterwards, he started celebrating. Before he went home, he visited John Eye's Moonshine Emporium up Snakeroot Hollow and got himself a jug of that establishment's finest brew. It was good stuff. I know that for a fact because I later used it in my rocket propellant (See *Rocket Boys*).

Buddy didn't go home to his wife and children that night. He went howling at the moon instead. He ended up in the Club House, the big old mansion Mr. Carter had built for his son that had been turned into sort of a hotel for Coalwood's single miners. Buddy roared inside and bumped around the parlor, bragging on who he was and what he was about to do.

"I was the best halfback in this state, and now I'm the best continuous miner operator there is, boys!" he yelled. He tripped over a chair and threw up near the fireplace. It was a sorry spectacle, and the miners who witnessed it agreed that Buddy had managed to get himself a bit puffed up. It was clear that something needed to be done about it. The only problem was that Buddy was a husband and a father. His parents still lived in Coalwood, too. Whatever was done couldn't embarrass his family. A few of the men wrapped Buddy up in a blanket and tossed him in a car and sped off. Another man was sent for my father.

It was late, and I should have been asleep, but I was up, listening to the little radio I had in my room. I had built it myself. It was a short-wave radio and I could hear voices from all around the world. This was in 1958 when I was fifteen years old and just beginning to imagine myself living and working in the outside world. It was an exciting thing for me to stay up late at night and listen to those low murmurs from the rest of the planet. I heard the knock on the back door. Mom and Dad and Jim had long since gone to bed so I answered the knock, finding a young man standing on the back steps, his cap in his hands. I recognized him as one of the miners who lived in the Club House. At his request, I went after Dad, who came downstairs in his pajamas. "Sir, we've got a problem with Buddy," the man on the steps told him. "We need for you to come and see."

Dad didn't say much of anything except to agree to go. He dressed quickly and grabbed his hat and coat. I did, too. He glanced at me as I climbed into the passenger seat of his old Buick but he didn't order me out. I just wanted to see what was happening. I guess it was the old reporter in me, the boy who'd founded the defunct *Coalwood News*.

Dad followed the miner's car down Main Street and through the center of town, the area we called Coalwood Main. This was where the Club House was, the main company store that we called the Big Store, the general superintendent's house, the Community Church, and the machine shops. We kept going, past the doctor's house, and down into Middletown and past Mudhole Hollow where Reverend Richard's church guarded the entrance. We kept going and turned at the fork in the road just before Frog Level and headed for a piece of wilderness called Big Branch.

The road had turned to dirt and was rutted, but still we bumped along. It was winter and Dad had to turn on the heater to ward off the bitter cold of the nighttime mountains. At last, the car in front pulled in at a clearing. I recognized where we were. During the summer, Coalwood kids used this part of the creek for a swimming hole. A beaver family had dammed it up for us. Ducks liked to be there, too, and deer would come down from the hills for a drink. You could catch some suckers and a few trout out of it, too. But during the winter, it mostly had a skin of ice over it. Surrounded by skeletal hardwoods, it was a dismal place.

In the headlights of the assembled cars, Buddy looked like a drowned possum. He sat on a rock beside the little pond, his head in his hands. What skin I could see of him was nearly purple. Men stood around him. I knew pretty much what everybody did in the mine, and I recognized them all as continuous miner operators. They were all taking turns having a word with Buddy. Dad stayed back, just outside the circle of light. I stood beside him.

"You have to get in there careful-like," a man was saying. "You can't push too hard, get ahead of your roof crew. If you do, you'll get slate down on top of you, get yourself messed up along with all the men at the face."

"Yes, sir," Buddy said, although it was in a stutter. His teeth were chattering pretty hard. He'd somehow gotten a really good dunking in the pond. It looked like he'd stayed in there for a long time, too. He also looked like he could sure use a blanket thrown over him, but nobody had quite seen fit to do it. He just sat in his wet clothes and shook from the cold.

"An operator's got to come to work ready to work," somebody else said. "They can't be out getting themselves drunk up before a shift."

I heard another voice I recognized. I knew everybody there, had known them all my life. "You got to be as careful with your missus and your kids as you are at the face," he said. "You can't be no hell-raiser, not no more. You got to be as good as your job."

Another familiar voice said, "You got to go at it, quiet-like. You get too big for your britches, too sure of yourself, that's when that roof is going to get you."

"Or you'll cut a pillar too close and it'll blow itself up, take you home to heaven."

"Make your wife a widow and your kids an orphan."

"And your mama and daddy ashamed they raised somebody so dumb."

"A man what's puffed up is a dead man in that mine."

"Yes, sir, yes, sir," is all that Buddy said, over and again.

At last, the men stopped and turned toward Dad. "You want to say something, Mr. Hickam?" somebody asked. It was as if all that had gone before didn't count unless my father, the man who'd given Buddy his new responsibilities, put a cap on the proceedings.

"Just one thing," Dad said. He searched the eyes of each man, then let his gaze fall on Buddy. Buddy looked up, expectantly. "I put each of you men here in this job because I was certain you could do it. You've never let me down. You've not let me down tonight."

Dad's eyes lingered on Buddy until the boy dropped his head and nodded. Buddy went to work the next day and was as good a continuous miner operator as Coalwood ever had. He didn't brag anymore, either. He didn't have to. He knew that he was among the best of the best.

We don't get puffed up.
We are proud of who we are.
We are not afraid.

OTHER VOICES: WE ARE PROUD OF WHO WE ARE

The Coalwood I Remember
Eleanor Marie Dantzler Siebert

My father, Mr. Devotie Dantzler, was the general manager of the stores owned by the Coalwood coal company. He worked hard to make his stores a positive force in the life of the community. He extended credit to families and worried when customers couldn't make their payments. He demanded the best from the people who worked for him, but he was kind and caring. He was proud of his part in spearheading the community effort to improve the Coalwood school playgrounds. He gave jobs to young people; not as an encouragement to stay in Coalwood, but as a means to find better lives. My mother, Eleanor Marie Dantzler (the first!) was a strong-willed woman and, in many respects, an early feminist. When she decided to work outside the home teaching music, she did it. She never indicated that there were limits on the professions that my sister and I could pursue. I became a chemistry professor at Mount St. Mary's College in Los Angeles. My sister Zanice "Ginger" Muckler became a professional singer.

Why was Coalwood special? The people who guided and looked over us, the hills that we played in, the time growing up when a child's world had a secure closeness but also freedom and open space for adventure—and the values: hard work, caring, teamwork and respect for the dignity of people doing their best. This is the Coalwood I remember, and it continues to inspire me today.

Our Way of Life
Bill Marshall

I saw a lot of strength and courage in Coalwood. Our dads were miners, and we knew they were in danger every time they went underground. One thing stands out in my memory: seeing the olive green company ambulance going toward the mine. All we could do was watch. We didn't know if someone had been hurt or possibly killed. Our moms gathered along the fence to comfort each other until news was received concerning what had happened. I'll never forget that. It was very hard to learn to live with the dangers of mining, especially as you grew older and realized how dangerous it was by listening to the men talk about their adventures in the mine. But it was our way of life in the coalfields, and with the strength and courage that our parents taught us, we learned to go on with life the only way we knew.

Pieces in Time
Fonnie Holder Klein

I remember playing chase, kick-the-can and hide-and-go-seek with neighbor kids under Caretta #5's one streetlight. I remember getting scared and running from the dad's honeybees when they were swarming on the tree limb and thinking how strong they were to hold on to each other in such a large group. I remember smelling freshly dug ginseng and gathering poke for dinner. I remember I was taught that if I put a short blade of grass between my thumbs, closed my hands together, then blew between my thumbs, it would create a whistling sound. I remember using grass and weeds to weave a "grasshopper's house" and catching and slightly squeezing a grasshopper so it would "spit tobacco." I also remember chasing and catching the floating white fluffs of dandelions. We called the white fluffs "fairies," and when we caught one we could make a wish. We also caught "lightning bugs" and put them in a jar with holes in the lid so they could breathe. I can still remember walking up a hollow and being surrounded by hundreds of different varieties of butterflies.

I remember visiting Dad in the hospital after he was hurt in a mine accident in Coalwood. The slate fell on him, hurting his legs and cutting off his nose, ear and lips. He got up and held his face together as he walked out of the mines. Doctors sewed everything back together, and Dad came home trying to breathe with black lung disease and scar tissue in his nose. He never asked us to feel sorry for him.

I'm proud to be an American and a coal miner's daughter. I learned this from my experiences growing up in Caretta: that a mixture of exercise, hard work and playing was a natural unplanned gift of childhood. I learned respect for all life forms, be it a human, butterfly, grasshopper, bee, snake or ant. I learned prayer works and to trust in God if I am lost, sick, in danger or expecting the worst in a situation. I learned death is not forever because the soul survives. I learned that helping others in need is my choice and to expect anything in return is selfish. I learned helping others even while I am in pain strengthens me. I learned family members are most important, and I learned the importance of true friends. I learned going through hard times and trusting in God makes you stronger.

The Sixteens
Guylinda Cox Bailey

While growing up in Coalwood it never occurred to me how safe we were. You never heard of vandalism or much violence. The company provided most everything for the residents including an ambulance. My mom told me she started labor in a terrible snowstorm on March 3, 1942, and had to be taken to the Stevens Clinic Hospital in Welch in the company ambulance. She claimed the ambulance couldn't have made it across the mountain to Welch except it traveled behind the cinder truck. She wasn't afraid, though, and everything turned out fine.

There were a lot of people in Coalwood who made a big impression on me. One of them was Richard Anthony, who worked for the company store. Richard was a small black man who always had a big smile and was extremely polite. As I think back on the wonderful examples I had growing up of honesty, work ethics and manners, Richard is high on my list. Since my mother was a teacher, sometimes she would have to order her groceries over the phone. Richard would put her order carefully in boxes. Mom would leave the back door open, and Richard would come into our kitchen, put the boxes down and unload the things that were perishable into the refrigerator and leave the rest on the kitchen table. My mother and everybody in Coalwood trusted Richard completely.

My best friend when I was a girl was Eleanor Marie Dantzler. We spent a lot of time outdoors, riding bicycles together. We even formed our own club with just us two members. We collected dues of five cents each, put it in a jar and hid it across the creek under a little cliff to keep it safe. Eleanor's mother and my mother, Mary Alice Cox, were just the opposite of Eleanor and me. They were ladies who loved dressing up and keeping themselves immaculately groomed. Our mothers tried to make us into little replicas, but we resisted with great passion. I can still picture Mrs. Dantzler doing her housework in a dress, hose and pumps!

Mrs. Dantzler played the organ and piano at church and taught piano lessons in her home. She also took on the task of gathering a group of girls and teaching them to sing together. There were six of us: Jane Todd, Claudia Allison, Lynn Ridenour, Janice Taylor, Eleanor Marie and Guylinda

Cox (me). We came to be known as The Sixteens. We practiced at the Dantzler's house at least once a week. We had fun and learned a little music too. Mrs. Dantzler taught me to be neat and nice, which wasn't in my nature. The Sixteens eventually got so we could harmonize and sounded pretty good. After a while we began to perform at different churches and organizations.

I look back on those times as a wonderful experience of learning to love music, discipline, manners and appropriate behavior for a young lady. I still sing in our church choir and love all kinds of music. I have thanked Mrs. Dantzler many times for her patience and tolerance of me during that time. I still keep in touch with Eleanor even though we live cross-country from each other.

My Uncle Carlos
Libby Rakes Emler

I went to school at Welch High School just across the mountain from Coalwood. My grandparents lived in Hemphill, a coal mining camp a few miles from Welch. There they raised seven children on a miner's pay. The one I always thought of as an inspiration was my uncle, who was the third from the oldest. His name was Carlos. When he was seventeen and a senior at Welch High School, he was working part-time at a dry cleaners in Welch. He was loading clothing into one of the large drum machines one day and somehow his arm got caught between the drum and the outside of the machine. His right arm was wrung off just above the elbow. Of course, the dry cleaners paid the medical expenses and

offered him a job with them for as long as they were in business, but that was his only compensation. Unfortunately, the
company closed a few years later. But Uncle Carlos never
gave up. He did not feel sorry for himself, and he never
blamed anyone for the accident or the lost job. He always
said he had his whole life ahead of him, and he was going to
make the best of it and do whatever he wanted to do.

Uncle Carlos had several other jobs before he went to
work for another dry cleaners. I remember him driving that
stick-shift laundry delivery van and people commenting that
they didn't see how he could handle the gears the way he
did. He would just smile and say it was no problem. After
awhile, he went to work for the city of Welch as a dispatcher.
He was so proud of working with the police and fire depart-
ments. Uncle Carlos died in 1988 of cancer, and I only hope
and pray he knew how much his courage and will to overcome so many obstacles meant to me and to all who knew
him. But that was just the way people were in the coalfields.

They Were Just Good People
Carol Todd DeHaven

My parents, Ada and Ray Todd, married in the late 1930s
and raised my two brothers and me in Coalwood, West
Virginia. When he first went to work, Dad was employed as
a "slate picker" at the tipple. This involved picking the rock
out of the coal before it was dumped into coal cars. He was
subjected to a continuous cloud of dust as he worked. He
came home so black all you could see were the whites of his
eyes. When he was only thirty-three years old, he was

diagnosed with lung problems and had to enter a sanitarium. Mr. Jennings, the general superintendent, gave my mother a job running the movie theaters in Coalwood and Caretta to tide us over while Dad was sick. I guess you could say we were poor, but we never knew it. It didn't take too much to make us happy. When Dad got a little better, he returned to work at the mine and later was a foreman at the tipple. Dad never missed work even though his health was not very good. Mom and Dad participated in all aspects of life in Coalwood. Mom taught Sunday school and helped with the Girl Scouts. Dad loved softball and helped build a field for the town teams. My parents always took time to do things for the community. They were just good people who enjoyed helping others. That's the way most people in Coalwood were.

My brothers and I carried the *Welch Daily News* to subscribers all over town. I can remember trudging along in the deep snow with those papers, but sometimes I'd go riding on sleds with my friends, which would make my deliveries a little late. Nobody seemed to mind. I remember one summer when I accidentally threw the paper and it landed in John and Goldie Basso's flower box. It snipped off the tops of every flower in the box! I knocked on the door of the Bassos, but nobody was home. Later along my delivery, Mr. Basso caught up with me in his big car. He said for me to get in, and I did. He took me to his house, where I cleaned up the flower box and apologized to Mrs. Basso, who was very nice even though I'd killed her pretty flowers. Afterwards, Mr. Basso took me home. I didn't throw my papers near any more flower boxes for the rest of my paper delivery career! When I stop to think about it, so many people were good to me during those times. Coalwood was a great place to grow up.

WE ARE PROUD OF WHO WE ARE: A SUMMARY

The people of Coalwood walked their streets with a sure pride of who they were and why their town existed. With that certain knowledge in their heads, they had a built-in dignity that gave them strength and courage. They faced each day knowing that those around them faced the same dangers and were of the same purpose. They wore pride like a suit of armor but were careful not to let it weigh them down. False pride was something they avoided. They knew that with pride went responsibilities such as working hard to bring more glory to their town and people and not quitting even when things got rough. They made certain that their children also had the same strong attitude, one of the most important for the underlying assumption of town life:

We are not afraid.

If you are afraid of something in particular, or of nearly everything, one of the first things you need to do is to figure out who you really are. This doesn't mean to focus on the things about yourself that you don't like. It means to figure out where you stand in the long line of people and events that got you where you are. I am confident that if you take the time to do that, you're going to find yourself surprisingly impressed about who you really are. Simply by existing, you had to come from a long line of survivors who managed to get through perilous times, even more perilous than these today. And, not only did they survive, they had families who branched out and had other families. Your ancestors got through droughts and floods and arduous ocean crossings. They fought in wars, got beat down, only to stand back up again. Perhaps they were slaves but got themselves free through sheer will, courage and perseverance. Whatever they had to do, they did it, or you wouldn't be alive. They endured. And as they endured, so can you—and prosper, too.

We are proud of who we are. To be able to say it and mean it, you have to be part of something greater than yourself, some "we." That "we" can be your company, your town, your state or your country. If you're in the military, it can be your unit or service. It can also be your religion. But the best thing it can be is your family, your *people.* Read about and listen to the stories of all those who have come before you, and then write down and tell your own stories so that your children and all those who come afterwards will know who they are, too. Become connected with a greater self that will give you strength and allow you to say, with assurance:

> *We are proud of who we are.*
> *We are not afraid.*

#2

We stand up for what we believe.

The habits of fear and dread are manifested in many ways. Negativity, unreasonable anger and constant worry are a few of the more obvious symptoms. Another is being timid and avoiding confrontation of any kind, especially in defending your opinion. If you've fallen into this habit, perhaps you tell yourself it doesn't matter. After all, what difference does it make what a single individual thinks? One opinion isn't going to make any difference in the grand scheme of things, is it? Maybe it's better just to lie low and let others do the hard work of figuring out how things should be. This kind of thinking means you are afraid. It is one of the more insidious symptoms of fear and dread. It may seem harmless to act meek and mild and scuttle around like a little mouse, but it is actually very destructive to your sense of well-being and enjoyment of life. If you act as if what you think isn't important, it's the same as believing *you* aren't important. An attitude like that can squeeze the life right out of anybody.

The people of Coalwood could never abide somebody who wouldn't stand up for themselves. It didn't matter what the opinion was, it was the willingness to defend it that was admired. The way folks saw it, the wrongness of somebody's opinion could be fixed, but a lack of backbone was a tougher problem. I knew at an early age that Coalwood expected everybody in it to stand up and express what they believed, even in the face of stiff resistance. I was also taught, however, that standing up for yourself didn't mean you could be mean to other people. You could fight, but you had to fight fair. Those were the rules.

Coalwood's attitude toward making a stand was not a call to violence in any way. What people admired was not striking out physically but the willingness to try to convince others to a particular way of thinking. As a child, I learned from the adults I admired that it is the contest of ideas that changes minds, and it is that contest you should enter, not only so that you might change people's minds, but because it allows you to be a fully functioning part of the community. No organization, town or country can advance if everybody doesn't participate in the debate that shapes it. If you're not used to speaking up, if you've spent a lifetime letting others get their way or if you've convinced yourself that what you believe doesn't really matter, it's time to get rid of that way of thinking. It's just another habit of being afraid. As the people in Coalwood would say, "You need to get your head turned around."

My father often made decisions that he thought were the best for the mine and for the town. He heard out his foremen and his miners before he made his decision, but then he led by deciding what to do and giving out the orders necessary to make it happen. He was often roundly criticized for his decisions. He accepted that, understanding that people who make decisions are going to get criticized. It goes with the manager's job. More than once, a big part of Coalwood lined up against him. The union would hold meetings and denounce him. They'd make up signs and hold them aloft while marching in front of the mine. They often misspelled his name. They'd scrawl HICKMAN IS A RAT or HICK-HAM IS A BUZZARD. My mom would laugh and say they got the spelling wrong just to aggravate Dad. It was probably the truth. My father hated it when anybody spelled "Hickam" wrong, and everybody in Coalwood knew it. But Dad never worried much about what anybody thought of him, except for Captain Laird and my mom. He was sure the things he did were for the good of the mine and the town, and as far as he was concerned, that was all that mattered. Everybody knew that, too. He was respected for what he believed, even by the men who painted up the signs and misspelled his name. They were proud to have a boss who would stand up for what he believed. The truth is my dad was just as proud that his men were willing to stand up for what they believed, too.

My father and mother were great readers, as were most of the people in Coalwood. One of my father's favorite writers was John Steinbeck, a bit surprising because Steinbeck made no secret of his love for the labor movement in the United States. One day when I was twelve years old and picking around the bookshelves in the upstairs hall, I found a book by Steinbeck titled *In Dubious Battle*. I noticed it was pretty well-worn, a good sign that either Mom or Dad had appreciated it. I took it back to my room and settled down to read it. I discovered it was a novel about some men trying to get a union started among the fruit pickers in California. It wasn't too long before Dad found me with it. He took it from me, thumbed through it familiarly and then asked me what I'd learned so far. "Fruit picking's pretty hard," I allowed.

"What else?"

"The union guys have to work like the devil just to get people to join them."

"Do they seem like good men?"

I shrugged. "Sometimes. Not always."

"How about the farmers? The ones who own the fruit and fight the union men. Are they good men?"

"Most of them are real mean, I guess. But others seem okay." I wasn't sure what he wanted me to say.

Dad gave me a thoughtful look and then handed the book back to me. "Keep reading. I want to hear what you think at the end of it. Mr. Steinbeck's a fine writer and a pretty good teacher, too. That's why, every so often, I'll read this very book."

I was intrigued that this was a book that held my father's interest enough to read it more than once, so I kept reading, learning a lot about the early days of union organizing in the United States and the difficulties the union men had in doing it. Passions ran high on both sides, and sometimes there were even bloody battles. After I finished the book, I went to Dad and told him that's what I had gotten out of it.

Dad heard me with a subtle smile. "Well, that's what the story is about, all right," he said. "But what else did you learn? What about the union? Would you ever join one?"

I told him I sure would have if I was as bad off as those fruit pickers. The only way they could stick up for them-selves was to band together.

Dad nodded. "That's right. I'd have done it, too. But what if you were on the other side, had a company you were trying

to keep going? Would you be mad at the union guys for what
they were trying to do?"

"I might," I confessed, "but I think I'd understand them
better because I'd read this book. I could kind of put myself
in their place."

Dad gave me a rare grin. "Mr. Steinbeck has done himself
most proud then," he said. "He has let you put yourself in
another man's place. There's nothing better an author can
do. And that's why every so often, Sonny, I pick up this book
and read it again. It reminds me to put myself in the other
man's place when the union comes around. I think we get
along better because of it."

Sometimes, the union would send their chief, a man I
called John Dubonnet in the Coalwood trilogy, to talk things
over with my dad. Both Dad and Mr. Dubonnet were more
than willing to stand up for what they believed, and in no
uncertain terms. Many times, I heard them arguing down in
the living room about the company and the union until my
mom went in and made them stop. She helped them make a
kind of peace with her offerings of coffee and cookies. Mr.
Dubonnet and my parents had known each other in high
school and had graduated together. Since they'd dated once,
I kind of think Mr. Dubonnet still liked my mom in a special
way, and she liked him, too. But there was never any doubt
that, in a pinch, she'd come down on my dad's side. I think
that quietly amused Mr. Dubonnet. For his part, Dad
respected Mr. Dubonnet although he rarely agreed with him
about much of anything. But after the arguments were done
and the union chief was gone, Dad would sometimes go and
sit on the porch and ponder things while looking at the
tipple grounds, just up the road. More than once, after a bit

of concentrated pondering, he rose from his chair and went to the mine phone, the black phone as we called it, and call and modify an order he'd given to get it closer to what the union wanted. Mr. Dubonnet had stood up for what he believed, and Dad had listened. Every so often, Dad would also change Mr. Dubonnet's mind, and he would be brave enough to go back and try to convince his membership. Dad and Mr. Dubonnet were both stubborn men who liked a good fight but, in the end, they did what was right for the men who depended on them and the town at large. As men of courage, they never failed to act with honor. I think because they knew in their hearts that both of them were fighting for the same thing, they came to respect each other, maybe even like each other in their own stolid way.

The key to being able to stand up for yourself is to first be certain of what you believe. It's hard work, sorting out all your experiences and education and what you see and hear to figure out what you think about things. Read, talk to people and really pay attention to what they say. Don't be fooled by the easy answer. Make sure you understand why you think the way you do. If you work hard to have an opinion, you're much more likely to fight for it. You will have the courage to tell others what you believe, and when you do that, you defeat fear.

I look back now with wonder at those people who built Coalwood and raised my generation. Every day, they lived and worked with the confidence of knowing who they were and what they believed. And when put to the test, there was little doubt about what they would do. They'd fight for their opinion.

We stand up for what we believe.
We are not afraid.

WE STAND UP FOR OURSELVES

People who are always afraid try to blend into the background, hiding in anonymity, or being so meek and mild as to appear nonexistent. No one could ever accuse my mom of being meek. A few months after she married my father and moved to Coalwood, she decided she should have a bathtub in her house. And not only should she have a bathtub, she should also have hot water to go in it. When she made her wishes known to her new husband, the young man who would become my father, he told her she should be happy just to have running water. That was more than most women in coal camps had. She could heat up her water on the coal stove, just like everybody else. As for a fancy bathtub, well, a washtub had been good enough for his mother and he guessed it was good enough for his wife.

Elsie Hickam heard Homer Hickam out, then headed for Coalwood Main. There, she went inside the office of Mr. Carter, the founder of the town. When told he didn't see the wives of miners, Elsie Hickam said she guessed he'd see her because she wasn't leaving until he did. The secretary picked up the phone and called the mine. Soon after, my future father, his face black with coal dirt, arrived in a fluster. "Elsie, you got to come on home," he said. "You're going to get me fired." Mom responded, in a loud voice, so that even God and Mr. Carter could hear it, "Homer, you're as good a miner as this old company's got, but even if you weren't, you deserve

to have hot water in your house. It isn't civilized. A man like
Mr. Carter, he knows that. Somebody just needs to tell him
out loud."

Dad tried to hush her, but nothing was going to hush Elsie
Hickam that day. After a bit, the door to Mr. Carter's inner
sanctum swung open and there stood the great man himself.
He was all dressed in black, with a high-collared shirt. His
face was angular and thin, and his expression was angry. At
the sight, Homer Hickam's face turned pale even under its
layer of coal. Mom just gave Mr. Carter a quiet stare.
Coalwood's boss of bosses crooked his bony finger at her.
With a sidelong glance at her husband, she walked inside.
The door swung shut with a terminal click of the latch. My
father sat down, a stunned look on his face. His career, such
as it was, was over, of that he had little doubt. Thirty minutes
later, the office door swung back open and Elsie Hickam
walked out. In the brief moment before his secretary closed
the office door, Homer saw Mr. Carter sitting at his desk,
looking grim.

In silence, Homer and Elsie Hickam walked home. At
their house, Dad could stand it no longer. "What did Mr.
Carter say?" he demanded.

Mom gave him a smug look. "He said nobody ever com-
plained about not having hot water before. I told him in that
case I could get a hundred more ladies who would be happy to
express that opinion. He said if he did it for me, he'd have to do
it for everybody. So I said, well, that's what he ought to do. He
said he guessed he ought. And that's what's going to happen. I'm
also getting my bathtub."

You could almost hear Dad's teeth grind. "You have
embarrassed me all over this town," he said. "Remember,

Elsie, it's the nail that sticks up that gets hammered."

Mom's response to that was, "Homer, if you think you're a nail, I guess you *should* get hammered."

Homer Hickam had no answer, and even if he had, he knew he'd get nowhere with his young bride, mainly because she was right. She'd stood up for herself, which was right and proper to do, even for a woman. The next day, Mr. Carter sent two plumbers to install a coal-fired hot water heater and put in a bathtub and do anything else Mom told them to do. There was no retribution on Dad except that he was mortified when Mr. Carter had fun telling everybody in town what a pistol that Elsie Hickam was. When hot water heaters got installed in every house in town, it wasn't the end to it. Pretty soon, there wasn't a wife who wasn't thinking about what else might be done to improve Coalwood, such as perhaps a better selection of groceries in the company stores. Mom had started something that never really stopped after that, the inclusion of women's thinking into the decision-making process of the town.

Sometimes, standing up for yourself is a matter of overcoming a natural inhibition. Still, it needs to be done, even when the result can be big trouble. The story of Marvin the card player was a good example of that.

This happened around 1952. I was nine years old at the time and even though my newspaper was long defunct, I was still interested in what everybody in town was doing. Marvin was interesting to me, mainly because he was different. He was a bit on the pudgy side and had worried little eyes. Considering the big, tough men who filled the town, he was not your standard coal miner. Still, Captain Laird needed somebody to work separating coal and slate in the tipple, and the only person who was willing to do it was Marvin. So the little man was hired.

Slate-picking was hard, nasty work. All day, a man had to bend over a belt and pick out slate and coal with too much rock in it before the good coal was sorted into different sizes for shipment to the steel mills. Marvin was good at the job and worked diligently, but it didn't take too long before it was discovered he was pretty good at figuring numbers. The Captain needed a clerk more than he needed a slate-picker, so Marvin was transferred to one of the grimy offices at the tipple as a trainee assigned to fill in the myriad company ledgers. Marvin proved to be a good clerk, although he wasn't much for conversation.

If Marvin had one thing going for him, it was his ability to play cards, especially bridge. When bridge games were held at the Club House, Marvin and his partner always won. He had an uncanny ability to figure out what cards the other players held. He was just as good at poker and won a fair amount of money from anyone foolish enough to play him. Although he rarely left town, somehow he found a girl over in Berwind to marry. Her name was Cora. Marvin and Cora were assigned a house up in New Camp, and soon they had themselves a daughter they named Stella.

In 1953, bridge was sweeping the nation as a great fad, and McDowell County had caught the fever. Bridge teams were organized by the coal companies, and games between opposing companies were scheduled. Pride was the reward for the winners. A countywide tournament was proposed, and Captain Laird accepted the challenge. He told everybody that Coalwood, like everything else it did, would be the best at bridge, too. Accordingly, the Captain turned his gaze on Marvin, who was summoned to the Captain's office. Hat in hand, he entered at the Captain's booming invitation. The Captain explained what Marvin would be doing the following weekend. "I shall play opposite you, of course, since I'm the second-best bridge player in town," the Captain apprised him. "With us together, the other companies won't stand a chance."

Marvin meekly thanked the Captain for his confidence but also said that he couldn't do it.

The Captain was taken aback. "Why not, man? Coalwood pride is at stake!"

Marvin blurted, "Because my wife won't let me! She hates cards." Then he just stood silent, his legs trembling. "A man that won't support his company and his town is not a man to be trusted!" the Captain roared. Then the Captain fired Marvin, and the little man fled.

Marvin wasn't a member of the union and had nowhere to turn. He walked home and told his wife Cora what happened. What she said is not recorded, but the gossip-fence nearly burned down from the news. Not many people supported Marvin. What was wrong with playing a little bridge for the glory of the town? Good riddance, a lot more added. Marvin and Cora had no friends to back them up. Well, maybe they had one. His name was Batto Patsey.

Batto Patsey was one of the many Italian immigrants in town. The one thing about Batto Patsey, my mom always said, was that he had a strong sense of justice. In Marvin's case, he was about to prove it.

When a man was fired in Coalwood, he was given two weeks to leave his company-provided house. The same was true for his family if he was killed. Houses were in short supply, and the new miner hired to replace the old one had to have a place to live. That was simply the rule. If he was going to help Marvin, Mr. Patsey would have to act fast.

Mr. Patsey went to Marvin and told him he had to make a stand. "How can I do that?" Marvin wondered, gulping at the very thought of standing up for himself.

"The Captain has a meeting with all his foremen every Friday morning," Mr. Patsey told him. "You have to come in and defend yourself in front of them."

Marvin was terrified. He'd made a life for himself in Coalwood by being quiet and meek. He moaned and said, "I'll be kicked out before I open my mouth!"

"It will take nerve, Marvin," Mr. Patsey acknowledged. "But you have to do it. I'll tell the Captain I invited you, but otherwise you're on your own."

Not an hour after Mr. Patsey had left his house, the news was all over town that Marvin was going to stand up to the Captain. Instantly, Marvin's stock went up. When he went to the post office, the postmistress smiled at him, a rare event. She'd have given him extra mail if she could have found some. Tough miners, chewing tobacco and gossiping on the Big Store steps, stood up and took off their hats as he went by. One of Coalwood's teachers told him in the Big Store how much she liked Stella in her class and was glad that now she wouldn't have to leave. Marvin was mystified at the reaction of everybody in town. He hadn't yet done anything, and they were all treating him like he was a hero. When Marvin got home, he told Cora about it and she replied that the neighbor ladies on both sides of their house had brought over covered dishes for supper. "They asked me to join their garden club, too," she said in wonder. "And they asked if I would help with the spaghetti supper at the school next month." Marvin noticed that Cora seemed pleased.

Marvin thought about it for the next couple of days. He hadn't yet done anything at all, but he felt infused with strength just because everybody thought he was going to stand up for himself. He decided he had to do it. He arrived at the Captain's office on Friday morning and went inside where the foremen had all gathered. The Captain, fully alert as to what was going to happen, glowered from behind his big desk. He called the meeting to order. "You have something to say to me, Marvin?" he boomed.

Marvin allowed as to how he did. "I have decided to play bridge for you, Captain."

Surprised, the Captain straightened in his chair. "Well, that's fine, Marvin."

Marvin kept going. "I've decided to play bridge for you, Captain, because I want to, not because you fired me when I said I wouldn't. I will play bridge for you, but then my family and I will leave Coalwood. I would not work for a man who would fire someone for such a trivial thing."

There was a murmur of approval from the assembly of foremen while the Captain's mouth fell open. "Why, Marvin, did you think I fired you? I think I said you're to change jobs. Why . . ." It was clear the Captain was thinking fast. "Why . . . there's a position for you down at the main office where you might learn a little accounting. I was hoping you might take it."

"I did not misunderstand you, Captain," Marvin replied in even tones. Most of the foremen thought he seemed to be a bit taller than they recalled. "You fired me for not playing bridge with you, plain and simple."

The Captain gave in. "You have me, Marvin. I'm a rank old rascal, that's for sure. But you have my respect, sir, like few others. I beg you to take your old job back—no, by gum, that new job down at the main office—and I don't expect you to do a thing for it, neither play bridge nor anything else. This old town, this old company, isn't a thing unless we have men like yourself working for it."

According to the story I heard at the kitchen table that night, Mr. Patsey had a huge grin on his face during the entire proceedings. "The thing about it is," Dad said, "a man who stands up for himself can't lose, no matter what else might happen."

"That goes for women, too, Homer," Mom said sweetly, no doubt savoring the time when she got her bathtub and her hot water heater. Mom was never one to forget such a thing, or to let Dad forget it, either.

As I grew up and went through life, I came to understand that it is never a bad thing to stand up for yourself, man, woman and child, too. If you do, you gain the respect of everyone, as long as you do it in an honest and respectful manner. That was the key for Marvin and the key for Mom when she went to see Mr. Carter. Not only did they make their case, they did it using words of respect. Respect is one of the keys to winning any argument. Being meek, however, does nothing except to get you mostly ignored.

By the way, not that it matters, but the Captain and Marvin won the county bridge tournament for Coalwood, and Marvin eventually got to be chief clerk for the company.

> *We stand up for ourselves.*
> *We stand up for what we believe.*
> *We are not afraid.*

675705886Z

READER/CUSTOMER CARE SURVEY

We care about your opinions. Please take a moment to fill out this Reader Survey card and mail it back to us.
As a special **"thank you"** we'll send you exciting news about interesting books and a valuable **Gift Certificate**

Please PRINT using ALL CAPITALS

BA1

Name
First   MI.☐   Last
                                                       Name

Address

City   ST ☐   Zip

Phone # (☐☐☐) ☐☐☐ - ☐☐☐☐   Fax # (☐☐☐) ☐☐☐ - ☐☐☐☐

Email

(1) Gender:
○ Female
○ Male

(2) Age:
○ 13-19   ○ 40-49
○ 20-29   ○ 50-59
○ 30-39   ○ 60+

(3) Your children's age(s):
Please fill in all that apply.
○ 6 or Under   ○ 15-18
○ 7-10   ○ 19+
○ 11-14   ○ 2   ○ 4+

(8) Marital Status:
○ Married
○ Single
○ Divorced / Widowed

(9) Was this book:
○ Purchased For Yourself?
○ Received As a Gift?

(10)How many HCI books have you bought or read?
○ 1   ○ 3
○ 2   ○ 4+

(11) Did this book meet your expectations?
○ Yes
○ No

(12) How did you find out about this book? *Please fill in ONE.*
○ Personal Recommendation
○ Store Display
○ TV/Radio Program
○ Bestseller List
○ Website
○ Advertisement/Article or Book
○ Catalog or Mailing
○ Other _____

(13) What FIVE subject areas do you enjoy reading about most? *Rank only FIVE. Choose 1 for your favorite, 2 for second favorite, etc.*

	1	2	3	4	5
Self Development	○	○	○	○	○
Parenting	○	○	○	○	○
Spirituality/Inspiration	○	○	○	○	○
Family and Relationships	○	○	○	○	○
Health and Nutrition	○	○	○	○	○
Recovery	○	○	○	○	○
Business/Professional	○	○	○	○	○
Entertainment	○	○	○	○	○
Sports	○	○	○	○	○
Teen Issues	○	○	○	○	○
Pets	○	○	○	○	○

FOLD HERE

BA1

9396058864

(25) Are you:
○ A Parent?
○ A Grandparent

(18) Where do you purchase most of your books?
Please fill in your top TWO choices only.
○ General Bookstore
○ Religious Bookstore
○ Warehouse / Price Club
○ Discount or Other Retail Store
○ Website
○ Book Club / Mail Order

(20) What type(s) of magazines do you SUBSCRIBE to?
Fill in up to FIVE categories.
○ Parenting
○ Sports
○ Fashion
○ Business / Professional
○ World News / Current Events
○ General Entertainment
○ Homemaking. Cooking, Crafts
○ Women's Issues
○ Other (please specify) _____

WE STAND UP FOR THE LEAST OF US

One way to get out of the habits of fear and dread is to take up for those who can't take up for themselves. There is always someone who needs your help. How can you be afraid if you're the protector of someone else in a dangerous world? Sometimes, just acting brave is enough to make you brave. But there's a double responsibility here. It isn't enough just to stand up for someone who needs your help. You also have to help teach that person to stand up for himself, too, so that he can keep his dignity. That was one of the great lessons I learned in Coalwood. I observed my parents and the other adults in town, especially our teachers, protect those in their midst who, through no fault of their own, were unable to always keep up. They were sometimes referred to as "the least of us," but they weren't thought of as anything but full citizens. Much was expected from "the least of us," too. A girl in my class I will call Novella was an example of that very thing.

Novella came from one of the most respected families in Coalwood. Her father was a loading machine operator and one of the best at what he did. Everybody liked him and thought his wife was a fine person. He had several sons and daughters, all of whom were smart and handsome. But there was a problem when Novella, their youngest daughter, came along. There was something wrong with Novella. Novella was a stout little girl with an oddly misshapen face. She had a pug nose, her thick lips sagged and her small eyes always seemed to be looking out into the distance. She had poor skin, which always seemed to be breaking out into sores. Her voice had kind of a guttural quality to it, and she had trouble forming words and making herself clear. It was a natural thing for the kids in her class to want to keep clear of her. I wasn't any different. I didn't know what had happened to her to make her the way she was, but whatever it was, I didn't want it to happen to me.

My first-grade class was so big that it had to be divided into two rooms, each with about thirty students. Mrs. Williams got one class and Mrs. Stapleton got the other. I was in Mrs. Stapleton's class and so was Novella. I ended up being seated behind her. It seemed, in fact, that every time we queued up for anything, I was put next to her. I tried to talk to her once or twice, but I couldn't understand what she said. She always talked with her head down, her words just mumbles. I couldn't figure her out. Mostly, I was scared of her and I didn't even know why.

One thing I had trouble figuring out was why Mrs. Stapleton never treated Novella any different from any other child in her class. Once we got to reading, we'd sit in a circle and everybody would read a line or two aloud from our books. When it was Novella's turn, she would read a little, but when she reached a word she didn't know, which didn't take long, she didn't try it. She just sat there. Mrs. Stapleton would wait a decent interval, then say the word and then make all of us say the word, even though it was usually an easy one. I didn't think it was right that everybody had to pretend we didn't know a word just because Novella didn't know it. We were all being slowed down by Novella. That was the way I saw it, and it made me mad.

Some days, Mrs. Stapleton would have everybody in class pair off and work together, to read or print something, to do some finger painting, or maybe make something out of modeling clay. I was nearly always put with Novella. From the beginning, I did all the work, and she just copied what I did. When Mrs. Stapleton came to look at what we'd done, Novella got the same praise I did. I began to really dislike Novella. It wasn't fair that I had to do the work and she got as much credit as I did. Nothing about the way Mrs. Stapleton treated Novella was right or fair in my opinion, and I thought something ought to be done about it. You have to understand I was only five years old at the time. The Coalwood School had a rule that if a child didn't wet his pants or cry too much, he could go to school a year early. As soon as I qualified in all respects, Mom pushed me out the door and told me to follow my brother to school.

I waited one night until Dad had gone into the living room to read the newspaper and brother Jim had gone off to play with his friends out in the dark somewhere. Mom was washing dishes. I asked if I could dry them, and after she got over the shock, she said, "Sure. Have at it," and handed me a dish towel. I took a swipe at a dish and then voiced my complaint about Mrs. Stapleton and Novella and the awful way I was being treated because I had to help her all the time and didn't get a bit of credit for it. When my little exposition was completed by a suggestion that perhaps my mother should have a word with my teacher about the situation, Mom stopped washing the dishes, slowly dried her hands and then snatched me by my shoulder so fast I couldn't get away. Her eyes were afire. "I am ashamed of you, Sonny Hickam," she said. When I looked away, she turned my head back to face her. "But I am also proud that you have been chosen to do a good thing. God know why Mrs. Stapleton picked you, but take it as a blessing. I do." Then she let me go. I went back to drying the dishes and tried not to sniffle too much. I didn't see what I'd done that was so wrong. As it turned out, my little talk with my mother got part of what I hoped for. Mom went to Mrs. Stapleton, all right, but not to complain. Instead, she made certain Novella and I were more or less joined at the hip for the remainder of my first-grade experience.

After Christmas vacation, I arrived at school and found Novella wasn't there. Mrs. Stapleton told the class that Novella was sick and that she was going to a hospital. Mrs. Stapleton didn't tell us what had made Novella sick, but I didn't much care. I didn't have to do Novella's work for her, that's all I knew. To my joy, I found myself paired off with Linda DeHaven, a bright, cheerful young lady. Linda and I had a lot of fun. Cute as a button, she was mischievous and would hide my books when I wasn't looking. I'd do the same with her crayons. We giggled a lot and passed notes, once we learned how to print them out. But as time passed, I started to miss Novella. Linda D. never needed my help. She was smarter than me, and a lot of times I found out that I was getting credit for the work she'd done. It wasn't like it was with Novella. It suddenly came to me, the way things tended to do, that I got a lot of fun out of being the one who helped Novella.

I started to mope around about the whole thing. Mom caught me at it, my face as long as a cat's tail. Mom demanded to know what my problem was. Since I didn't know what it was, exactly, I asked her a question. "What's wrong with Novella, and when is she going to come home?"

Rather than answer, Mom asked a question of me in reply, an irritating habit. "Why would you care? I thought you didn't like her."

"I like her," I answered and then bared my soul. "I was just kind of afraid of her."

Baring my soul to my mother was never a sure thing in terms of her reaction. This time she thought that it was pretty funny, demonstrated by the fact that she laughed out loud. Then she said, "Novella is the nicest little girl God ever put on this earth. She wouldn't hurt you or anybody else. I swan, Sonny, where you get these strange ideas is beyond me. It's the Hickam in you, I suspect." (Swan, by the way, is what Coalwoodians used to say rather than "swear." To swear was like praying.)

Anytime I did anything Mom thought was odd, she accused me of having too much Hickam blood and not enough Lavender, her side of the family. It might have been true but it didn't solve my problem, whatever it was. That was my whole point, the one she didn't understand. *Why did I miss Novella?* After all, she hadn't been anything but trouble.

Then one day, Novella was back. I saw her round shoulders in the chair in front of me, and I perked right up. I wanted to tell Novella I was glad to see her, but somehow I couldn't get the words out. She looked tired and a bit scared. I guess she had a right to be both. Her absence had put her so far behind in school, I couldn't imagine how she would ever catch up.

At recess, Novella went off to sit by herself under a tree. Then, she got sick to her stomach and threw up. We all just stopped and stared at her. Usually, being the lowliest of the low, we were totally, utterly ignored by older kids but for some reason, a fifth-grade boy observed Novella and said, "She's nasty, isn't she?"

"No, she isn't!" Linda DeHaven cried out, and we all

joined her in a tinny uproar. Novella was our classmate, and we weren't going to let anybody else say something mean about her. "Get out of here!" we yelled, and a few of the braver first-grade boys made a rush at Novella's tormenter. The fifth-grader ran away.

I had a clean white handkerchief that I kept in my hip pocket. Mom gave me a fresh one nearly every day with the instruction that I was to keep it clean, a strange admonition, but one I tried to follow. Heedless of my mother's instructions, I took out my handkerchief and used it to wipe Novella's face. She mumbled her thanks, and all of a sudden I felt like crying. If the other boys hadn't been sure to call me a sister for it, I would have, too. I felt like crying because I was ashamed of the way I had felt about her before.

I walked with Novella back to class and couldn't wait until we got to work together. I started to not only enjoy doing the printing and the reading and the coloring and whatever we were doing together but also explaining, as best I could, how to do it. Mrs. Stapleton told us we were a good pair of workers, high praise in the Coalwood School. When it was time for the first-grade school play, she decided that Novella and I would stand up before the whole school and give a nonsense speech. The look on Novella's face was pure terror. Carefully, she formed her thoughts, saying each word as clearly as she could. "I can't do that, Mrs. Stapleton," she said. "I can't remember things."

"Yes you can, dear," Mrs. Stapleton said with complete confidence. "Sonny will help you." I found myself nodding eagerly.

Mrs. Stapleton gave us a half-hour every day to practice our lines. Novella and I would go up on the stage in the empty gymnasium and say what we were supposed to say. I'd say one line and then she'd say the other. She had trouble remembering, just as she said she would, but she really tried, and that was enough for me. Since I was so busy helping Novella, I completely forgot that it was pretty scary for me to stand up in front of the whole school, too.

Our first-grade play was a Tom Thumb wedding. I played an usher, and Novella played a flower girl. After that, we did our little nonsense speech. I still remember part of it:

Ladies and Jellybeans, we stand before you to sit behind you to tell you about something we know nothing about. It's about George Washing-Machine who crossed the Missi-sloppy River to sign the Declaration of Indigestion. . . .

It was really a nonsensical rhyme, but somehow that made it easier to say in front of all the big kids and the adults in Coalwood. We got lots of laughs. I liked it that even my dad laughed. When Novella forgot a line, I whispered it to her, but she didn't forget very many. At the end, we got huge applause. Novella and I bowed together, and when she straightened back up, I saw she had the most amazing smile on her face. I'd never really seen her smile before. All of a sudden, I realized what a delightful smile Novella had. She lit up the whole gymnasium with that smile. For the rest of the time at the Coalwood School, I was Novella's friend and did everything I could to help her in class and to watch out for her, too. It sure made me feel good to do it. As best I could, I was her protector, and in so many ways, it turned out she was mine, too.

If you want to get past fear and not get hooked on dread, find someone who needs help and give them everything you've got. Pretty soon, you'll find you won't have time to be scared!

> *We stand up for the least of us.*
> *We stand up for what we believe.*
> *We are not afraid.*

WE STAND UP FOR TOUGH TEACHERS

The people of Coalwood stood up for what they believed even when they noticed that the rest of the world didn't share their convictions. One of those beliefs was that teaching their children was too important to fool around with anything other than having tough teachers. In the 1950s, the modern theories of education were starting to become popular across the United States. Teachers were told they needed to learn how to "relate" to their students and to be friendlier. They were told that they should be "guides" or "facilitators" and should be more interested in stimulating their students than actually teaching them facts and figures. Schools were supposed to be "open" and "permissive" so that students wouldn't feel that they were oppressed. It might have been a fine idea for the rest of the country and even the world, but this was absolutely not the Coalwood way.

As a student with more than a little tendency toward laziness, I might have voted for those new theories, given half a chance to do it, but I never got that chance and neither would anybody else as long as George W. Bryson, the superintendent of McDowell County Schools from 1935 to 1968, held his job and drew breath. Mr. Bryson believed that the purpose of education was to teach students the things they would need to know so they could go out and get good jobs and be good citizens and live in a manner that added to their communities and gave glory to their families. Toward that end, Mr. Bryson's schools had a rigorous, demanding and precise schedule of classes, each one designed to build on the one that preceded it. He also staffed up with tough teachers. It was Mr. Bryson's belief that McDowell County students should be taught as if their very lives depended on what they learned in our schools, which, of course, it did.

Mr. Bryson had no greater supporters than the people of Coalwood. At every Parent Teachers Association meeting, the school was packed with parents and union and company officials. They heard from the principal and the teachers as to what was being taught and how it was being taught, although they already knew much of it, having thoroughly questioned their children after each school day. I rarely, if ever, got by with saying "nothing" as an answer about what I'd learned in school that day. Mom wasn't satisfied until she'd squeezed it all out of me, bit by bit. After awhile, I started paying more attention in school just so I'd have something to tell her.

The teachers of Coalwood were as dedicated a bunch as ever existed. The grade-school teachers were called the Great Six, a contraction of "grades one through six." The Great Six had been in their positions for a long time, and some said they'd been there forever. These ladies knew everything there was to know about their students before we ever entered one of their classrooms. They knew who our parents were, who our brothers and sisters were, and who exactly we were, too. They believed, more than anything, that it was absolutely, utterly necessary to intensely teach us the basics of education—reading, writing, grammar, literature and mathematics—without frills. When they observed a talent, they honed it as hard as they could until that talent shone like burnished gold. When they observed an educational weakness, they went after it like bobcats after a chipmunk. There was never any doubt that they were in charge of their classrooms, and if any of their students were so foolish as to question their authority, several layers of discipline were ready and willing to be applied, mostly including that of our parents. The Great Six and our parents treated our education as serious and vital, too important by far to ever coddle even one of us, no matter how fragile we might think ourselves, mentally or physically. They were convinced that students were engaged in the most serious of enterprises. If we didn't learn, we would not succeed or prosper for the glory of the people who had raised us. No child was allowed to disrupt a class, at least not for long. There was teaching to do and learning to accomplish. Time was too short to let anything slow the Great Six down.

Every so often, the mother of one of the Coalwood students would forget who she was and where she lived and go up against the Great Six. Mrs. Cleo Mallett was the one most likely to do it. As long as she lived in Coalwood, Mrs. Mallett always seemed to be harboring a grudge of one kind or another. She was judged a good woman by most people in town when they were feeling charitable, but there was no doubt she had a big blind spot when it came to her sons, one of whom was in my class. His name was Rodney, and we, his fellow classmates, were wary around him. He was a big-boned boy with a mean streak about a mile wide. Mostly, I thought of him as a thug. He liked to pull the pigtails of the girls and trip a boy now and again when one of us were going up to the blackboard. He wasn't above hitting you in the back when nobody was looking either. I detested Rodney, pretty much, and I wasn't by myself. The thing about it was, Rodney didn't care. He had no need of friends. He had his big brother, Siebert, who was built along the same lines with the personality to match. When those two were together and wandering around town on the weekends, there was almost always a brawl. My friends and I got in more than one rock-throwing, corn stob–swinging contest with them. Once, while I was riding my bike behind the post office, Rodney raced out from behind a car with a corn stob and knocked me silly. Roy Lee and Jimmy Evans and Benny Brown avenged me by tracking the boy down and throwing him in the creek, but I had a lump on the back of my head for a week.

One day, when we were in the sixth grade, Rodney decided he didn't care to go outside and dust the erasers even though it was his turn. Instead, he picked them up and went just outside the classroom and began pounding them on the lockers, sending a cloud of white chalk up and down the hall. Mrs. Lindley, our teacher, had the boy bent over so fast he was still holding an eraser when he received his first whack with her open hand on his backside. When Rodney arrived home that night, he told his mother that Mrs. Lindley had pounded him with a board. He limped around the house that evening to show how hurt he was. Mrs. Mallett came to the school the next morning loaded for bear, and Mrs. Lindley was the bear. She was going to sue, she told Mr. Likens, the principal, if Mrs. Lindley wasn't punished for damaging her son.

Suing in Coalwood was an unlikely proposition. You could threaten to do it, but it wasn't about to happen, seeing as how we had no lawyers in town and you'd have to go all the way to Welch to find one. That would mean letting county seat people get into Coalwood business, and not even Mrs. Cleo Mallett would countenance that. Nonetheless, Mrs. Mallett began to make noises all over town about what a mean and cruel person Mrs. Lindley was. Mrs. Mallett even made Leo, her husband, bring it up at one of the union meetings. Then the *Welch Daily News* got wind of the controversy and wrote up a little story about it. The article made it sound as if Mrs. Lindley had battered Rodney beyond all that was reasonable. You'd have thought it was lucky he'd lived, according to the reporter's breathless prose. The people of Coalwood were mortified that a member of the Great Six had been so pilloried in print. Things were clearly out of control and something had to be done.

Since Mrs. Mallett was the wife of a union man, it had to be union women who took care of the situation. They did it by holding a little party for Mrs. Lindley, a cookies, cake and punch party that showed up just before school was let out. About fifty ladies crowded inside our little classroom with all their goodies. They stuck around afterwards and cleaned up everything, and they also very pointedly went outside and dusted all of Mrs. Lindley's erasers. Mrs. Mallett had been invited to the party. She didn't go, but she heard about how it went, and she got the point. Her complaints directed toward Mrs. Lindley stopped, and she started complaining about something else. Rodney still continued to be trouble and still got the occasional whack on the seat of his pants from Mrs. Lindley and any other teacher who observed his little cruelties. When he went upstairs to the junior high school, he made the mistake of stealing money out of the cafeteria cashbox. Even his mother had no excuse for that. Rodney was punished by having to scrub the boy's room toilets for the remainder of the school year. The interesting thing about that was it turned out to be something Rodney was pretty good at doing. And once he had a sense of accomplishment, he turned out to be a pretty fair old boy. He ended up a janitor working for the federal government in Washington, D.C. I'm proud that Rodney turned out so well, but every so often, the back of my head still aches from that corn stob when he ambushed me behind the post office. I'm glad Mrs. Lindley gave him that whack. I only wished she would have hit him harder.

The teachers in the upper grades had the same teaching philosophy as the Great Six except for putting more responsibilities on their students. Junior high students were required to learn their schedule of classes, move promptly to them at the bell and were also assigned homework, rare in grade school. But once we were older and going upstairs to the junior high school, the teachers there worked to prepare us for our next steps into educational adulthood, that of going across two mountains to the town of War, where we would attend Big Creek High School.

The teachers at Big Creek were similar to our Coalwood teachers except they dealt with students from all over the district, not just from Coalwood and Caretta. My physics and chemistry teacher in high school was Miss Freida Riley.

Since my book *Rocket Boys* and the movie *October Sky* were released, Miss Riley has taken on near-icon status across the nation and the world. Wherever I go, I am thanked by people of all walks of life, but especially by tough teachers, for telling her story because they say it's their story, too. At long last, they say, someone has written about a real school teacher, one who not only fought for her students but insisted that they learn. It seems to be the latter observation that's the most important to these teachers. In *Rocket Boys*, I quote Miss Riley as saying, "All I've done is give you a book. You have to have the courage to learn what's inside it."

For those readers who haven't read *Rocket Boys*, here's why Miss Riley got us that book. After a lot of experimenting, the six boys of the Big Creek Missile Agency got good in our craft. We built up a body of knowledge, carefully writing down what worked and what didn't. All we needed was just a little help to get us into the ranks of the true rocket scientist. That was when Miss Riley got us a special book to help us learn how to properly build our rockets. The book she got for us was one designed for doctorate-level students in rocketry and required a working knowledge of calculus and differential equations. At the time, I confess I was having trouble with algebra. But we learned what we had to learn because Miss Riley said we could. Before we were done, we were using what we learned in that book to design and build sophisticated rocket engines. Our rockets were flying miles into the sky, and there wasn't a more professional group of rocketeers in the country, except for maybe those who were working for NASA. Six coal miners' sons had managed to become much more than anyone thought we could be just because we had a teacher who was willing to help us do it.

Note that she helped. She didn't do the work. We were expected to do that, and we did.

I first met Miss Riley in 1958 when I was in the tenth grade and she was a student-teacher. She had graduated at the top of her class at Big Creek, then gone to Concord College to get her teacher's certificate. Even though I'm certain she could have gone anywhere to teach, she came back to Big Creek. She was pert, and bright-eyed, with freckles sprinkled across her nose and sleek black hair. I think all the boys in her class were just a little in love with her. I know I was.

Despite being young and pretty, Miss Riley was a no-nonsense teacher. She came to class well prepared, and she expected her students to be just as ready. Although she was friendly and would engage us individually in conversation, it was clear that she was our teacher first and our friend second—a distant second. Miss Riley seemed to take an interest in me immediately, asking about my parents, asking me about my interests, wondering if the rockets I was building might be a good idea for a science fair entry. Her interest would ultimately lead the boys and I to try our luck with the science fairs at the county, state and national levels. We didn't do it for scholarships as the screenwriters had it in the movie about us. There were no scholarships involved. We entered those science fairs to make our parents, our hometowns and especially Miss Riley proud of us. Pure and simple.

In my senior year at Big Creek, Miss Riley became sick with Hodgkin's disease, an incurable cancer at the time. She didn't tell her students about it. She taught us about it. After gossip had spread around the school about her affliction, she took an extra moment with her students to teach us about her illness, even drawing a diagram on the blackboard on what part of the body it attacked. She asked for no pity, only understanding of what the disease was and how it worked. It was her problem, not ours. She'd fight her cancer, thank you very much. We were to do our jobs, and that was to be good students.

After I went off to the engineering school at Virginia Tech, I occasionally came back to visit Miss Riley in her classroom. Her Hodgkin's went into remission for some years and she continued her education at West Virginia University every summer. I last saw her a few weeks before I graduated from college. She was quite thin and looked very tired, but her eyes lit up at the sight of me! She was so proud that I was going to graduate. Miss Riley died while I was on military duty overseas. To the last, she taught, even when her students had to carry her by litter to her class. When I found out she was gone, I wished then that I had told her how much she meant to me.

Miss Riley was a lover of life. It is clear in her history. She read extensively, she played the piano expertly, she loved her family, and she loved her students. She was always just one inch away from a smile. In very many ways, that smile now lights up this nation and the world with the hope that we may once again find our way back to the old ways, the ways of duty and honor, the ways of our parents and our tough teachers.

Dr. Wernher von Braun, the greatest rocket scientist who ever lived, said, "All one can really leave one's children is what's inside their heads. Education, in other words, and not earthly possessions, is the ultimate legacy, the only thing that cannot be taken away." Miss Riley and all the tough teachers in McDowell County back in the 1940s and 1950s knew this lesson as well as Dr. von Braun. She and the teachers of Big Creek and the Coalwood School were tough because they needed to be. The results were dramatic. Of my high school graduating class, 80 percent of the kids from Coalwood and Caretta went on to college. It was a combination of caring parents and tough teachers that caused that result. Tough teachers should be considered American heroes. Without them, we as a nation simply will not learn what we need to survive. And when our teachers are tough and others complain about it, we need to remember to back them up. It is a matter of life and death for your kids that they be properly educated. If your children are taught by tough teachers, they'll learn more than math, grammar, reading, writing and history, too. They'll also learn a way of life, one that has no room for fear.

We stand up for tough teachers.
We stand up for what we believe.
We are not afraid.

WE STAND UP FOR THE HONEST MAN

A dishonest person is nearly always frightened. They lie to keep the truth at bay and use whatever verbal gymnastics they can to cloud the issue they are forced to confront. Conversely, an honest person is someone who isn't afraid of the truth and lays it out as simply as possible. It's easy to tell the truth teller because the truth is always simple. Lies have to be more complicated and use muddy logic. As soon as you have trouble following the reasoning of a fellow, you can pretty well figure they're lying about something. That means they're probably scared, too.

In Coalwood, we were taught to follow the honest man (which meant the honest woman, too) and to be honest ourselves. It was just the best way to live, and the simplest. This didn't mean, however, that we were supposed to use honesty like a club, brutally telling everyone exactly what we thought at the moment we thought of it. Besides being uncivilized and just plain mean, it was foolish and counterproductive to act like that. I was taught this lesson by my dad, although it sure wasn't his intention. For many years, my mother would rise well before dawn to prepare Dad's breakfast before he went off to work. One morning, he took a long look at her in her rumpled housecoat and something came over him. He never could figure out what it was, but something made him say, "You know, Elsie, you don't look so good in the morning." Mom, in the middle of scrambling up some eggs, put down her spatula, wiped her hands on her apron and replied, "Well, Homer, we can fix that," and she promptly went back to bed. She never got up and fixed his breakfast again. My mom was one for making a point, and I guess she made it. I don't think I ever heard Dad criticize the way Mom looked again, morning, noon or night. He sure told her how pretty she looked, though. But she still didn't get up and fix his breakfast.

Although Mom taught Dad a little bit about choosing his words carefully, or maybe not saying anything at all, at least about her, he was always certain to tell the absolute truth out loud at the mine. There, his word was taken as absolute, and when he said something was so, it was so. Dad's kind of honesty at the mine wasn't complicated. I remember him quoting the Captain. "Two honest men can solve anything. One liar can foul up the works." As far as Dad was concerned, the Captain had never said anything more true. A mine superintendent had to get the exact truth from his foremen at the end of their shifts each day. If the foreman gave false information, perhaps to make his section look better than another man's, it could cause wrong and perhaps even fatal decisions to be made. Honesty was one of the most prized characteristics of the men who worked in the mine. It was also the bond between the men who represented the company and the union when it came time to negotiate.

During the summer between my freshman and sophomore years in college, I joined the union and worked in the coal mine to help pay my way through engineering school (see *Sky of Stone*). When I met with him, I asked Coalwood's union chief why he disliked my dad. Mr. Dubonnet allowed that he didn't dislike him at all. He just didn't like his opinion about most things. "One thing about Homer, Sonny," he told me, "is that he is flat-out honest. I may not like much of what he says but, by God, if he tells you something, you know he believes it's the Gospel truth. I can work with a man's truth, and live with it, too. I'd hate to negotiate with a dishonest man. Pretty soon, I get to be dishonest, too. Dishonesty is contagious. Nothing can infect an outfit like a liar let loose in it."

Two honest men can solve anything. One liar can foul up the works. To get rid of fear, admire and support the honest person, and be one yourself.

We stand up for the honest man.
We stand up for what we believe.
We are not afraid.

WE STAND UP AGAINST BULLIES

Bullies are terrible creatures. They like to inflict pain and suffering, just for the enjoyment of causing it. They don't seem to have any sense of morality about what they do. Right is whatever they say it is. They're selfish, too. Usually, they're bullies because they're bigger, or meaner or have some advantage. Did I mention bullies are a rotten bunch? They're not just swaggering kids on the playground, either. Bullies can end up being your boss or a coworker or just about anybody in your life. The fellows who hijacked the passenger jets on September 11, 2001, and crashed them into the World Trade Center and the Pentagon were a bunch of bullies. They thought it was just fine to make other people suffer just so they could have their way. Such wicked, evil people are purveyors of fear. Their whole plan is to get their victims hooked on fear so it becomes an inescapable part of their lives. The best way to beat fear and beat terrorists is to refuse to be a victim, to stand up and fight.

The people of Coalwood could not abide a bully, at least not for long. Bullies had to be handled, and for the most part, it was expected that those being bullied would do the handling, thus making even that awful situation a positive experience. Sooner or later, however, if a bully didn't stop what he was doing, or the tormented couldn't figure out how to make him stop, Coalwood society stepped in and took care of it. It was the same as today when American society had to step in and stop the big bullies who sent their little bullies in a failed attempt to terrorize our country. It's enough to make you wonder why bullies do what they do. They never win, not in the end. They always become the most miserable of human beings without friends or respect. Maybe it's because deep down in their puny hearts, in the faraway places of their rancid little souls, bullies and terrorists are as stupid as they act.

Coalwood was a place where all of the kids knew one another. We came from different parts of town and tended to form groups based on our geographical locations or interests, but we had a common bond as Coalwoodians, one and all. As far as I knew, all the girls in town got along just fine. It was us boys who tended to fight. Fighting was seen as a normal boyhood activity and was condoned by our parents as long as it didn't get too rough. Our fighting wasn't usually done by fists or throwing rocks. Occasionally that happened, but usually we fought by choosing up sides and playing straight base or dodgeball or some other active game. Or we fought by pretending to be Cherokee warriors or cowboys and shot at each other with imaginary bullets and arrows, all in the name of fun. We'd build forts out of logs or snow and defend them against the other boys. We'd swing on grapevines to see who could swing the highest or climb sheer cliffs to see who was the bravest. Our fighting was usually done in positive ways that tended to wear us out before it ever got too serious. But when a bully appeared, fighting almost always got down to the most primitive of levels pretty quickly. Since I was small and nearsighted, I was a perfect target for a bully, especially since there was a built-in excuse to knock me around. I was, after all, the second son of the mine superintendent, a man who often made unpopular decisions about the mine and the town. When the union men went out on strike, it was a perfect time for a bully to come after me. Since I couldn't beat bullies physically, I had to learn to handle them, and I did, although it took me awhile to learn how.

Whenever I got beat up at school by a bully, I tried to hide it from my parents. Dad had enough problems at the mine, I figured, without me adding to them. I knew what my mom would say because I'd heard her say it. She'd see the blood on my shirt and know something had happened. She was a direct-action kind of person. She'd say, "Sonny, pick up a rock and when that old boy isn't looking, hit him as hard as you can with it and then run like heck." It wasn't bad advice, but it wasn't very practical. Bullies didn't tend to get caught in surprise attacks. They ran in packs, the other bullies always on the scout.

Of course, it eventually got around to my dad that I was being occasionally beaten up at school. One time, he lowered his newspaper when I strolled into the living room and asked me about it. I confessed it was true. After a moment of musing, he said, "You know, Sonny, if everybody was kind, there'd be no reason to be brave." Then he went back to reading his paper, leaving me to puzzle out how that solved my problem.

For some reason, it seemed the bullies in my class reached their zenith when we were in the fifth grade. There was a trio of them. I'll call them Floyd, Bert and Calvin, although those weren't their real names. I wasn't their only target, but I was a prime one. When I was caught behind the school building after classes were let out, they laid into me, tearing my new shirt and breaking my glasses. I would have run but they had me cut off. I couldn't hide the results from my mother. I needed new glasses, and they weren't cheap. She said she was going to the school the next day and put a stop to those bad boys, but I begged her not to do it. "I'll never be able to go back to school if you do," I explained. "I'll be called a sister because my mom had to come and take up for me."

Mom understood, or so she said. "Handle it," she also added, "before the whole family is shamed all over town."

I wanted to handle it, but I just didn't know how. I wished I could be more like my brother. Jim was in the class ahead of me, and even though we had the same father, he never had any trouble with bullies. I figured that was mainly because he was bigger than any of them, but there was something else about Jim, too, now that I thought about it. He carried himself in such a way that you just knew by looking at him, that he was not a boy to mess with. He had a swagger in his walk and his talk, and he was more than willing to back it up with his muscles, too. I considered my brother's example and then concluded it was hopeless. I could never be like my brother. I was stuck. How could I defeat Floyd, Bert and Calvin?

It was the Reverend Richard of the Mudhole Church of Distinct Christianity who gave me the key on how to fight them. When he spied me at the Big Store, he asked me how I did these days and I said I did just fine. Then he brought up the beating he'd heard I'd received, and I readily confessed to it. "Here's a proverb, Sonny," he said. *The wicked flee when no man pursueth; but the righteous are bold as a lion.* Be a lion, boy. Be a lion."

I considered the Reverend's advice. It was good advice, I was certain of it. I just didn't know what it meant, and I said so. It seemed I was always getting good advice I couldn't use. The Reverend was straightforward this time. "I mean for you to fight, Sonny. Fight and don't stop, especially when those old boys are ready to stop. That's the key to beating them. You have to go past when they're ready to stop."

I sorted it out, but I wanted to be certain I understood. "You mean keep fighting until Floyd, Bert and Calvin get tired, even though I'm getting the you-know-what kicked out of me?"

He nodded. "Wear them boys out. Keep going at 'em until they can't hold up their arms no more."

I pondered his advice and came up with what I considered a good question. "Won't that hurt?"

"Yes," he said enthusiastically. "It'll hurt those bullies so bad they won't ever bother you again."

I thanked the good Reverend and went off to think about what he'd advised. I was still thinking about the hurting part. I couldn't imagine how it would hurt those bullies more than me if I kept fighting them even when they were ready to stop. Would their fists get too tired?

I talked things over with Roy Lee and a few of my other buddies. They were willing to come to my defense, they said, but they didn't think that would stop Floyd, Bert and Calvin. "They'd just catch you by yourself some other time," Roy Lee said, and I knew he was right.

I even went to my brother. "You want me to knock them around?" he asked, with raised eyebrows. "Sure, I'd be happy to do that for my sister."

I got his point, loud and clear. I had to fight the bullies by myself. I kept thinking about the Reverend Richard's advice to fight past where Floyd, Bert and Calvin wanted to go, whatever that meant. Then it came to me in a flash, like things almost always did. I had to be unbeatable! No matter what those bullies tried, I couldn't ever let down around them! I had to keep on and never stop. I had to bring up all the energy I had inside me to make that happen. The next time I saw Reverend Richard, I told him what I had figured out. The Reverend said I had it right.

So I became a lion. I prowled the playground as a lion, alert, ready for trouble. I even took on the countenance of a lion, which I took to be one with a small smile, narrowed eyes and a firm jaw. When I did that, I noticed I was kind of walking and looking a bit like my brother, or at least a scrawny little four-eyed version.

I didn't look for trouble, but it eventually came anyway. This time I was caught walking home from a piano lesson. At the alley between the Big Store and the company offices, I was dragged off the street by my three tormenters and pummeled. As a lion, I fought back, feeling the lion's courage, its spirit, its energy. I was mostly ineffectual but as soon as I started resisting, I noticed immediately that Calvin backed off a bit. Floyd wasn't certain of me, either. Bert kept flailing but I didn't just take it. I flailed back. I ignored the pain of Bert's blows and got in a lucky hit of my own. Shocked, he stepped back to let the other two boys get in their licks. They knocked me down and took off my shoes, but I kicked Calvin in the head when they did it. They sat on me and twisted my arms and forced my face down into the dirt, but I never stopped squirming. Pretty soon, listening to them gasping for breath, I even started laughing. I wasn't hurt that much.

The bullies had given their best and were getting tired, but I was still going. They kept asking me if I gave up, and I kept saying no. When they got off me, I came up swinging. They were shocked. I could see it in their faces. And what a beautiful sight it was, too. It told me I had won. "You're crazy," Bert said when I came at them. Calvin and Floyd danced away. "He *is* crazy!" they cried.

They were right. I was crazy, crazy as a lion. Reluctantly, they took up the fight again. My nose was bleeding, and I made sure I got my blood on their clothes. Floyd started sniveling. "My maw is going to kill me, I got this shirt bloody," he said. "You ready to quit, Sonny?" I had him begging now.

"Never!" I yelled. "I'm not ever going to quit!"

Then the three of them started walking rapidly away from me. Shoeless, shirt nearly torn off and bleeding profusely, I chased after them. They looked over their shoulders and then started to run. I stopped but they didn't. *The wicked flee when no man pursueth; but the righteous are bold as a lion.* Those bullies never bothered me again.

To conquer a bully, you have to show that you're stronger than a bully, even if it's only to be mentally stronger. You have to think like a lion. You have to *be* a lion. Lions aren't scared. Lions don't fear, and they don't dread, either. Lions keep their heads up and their hearts strong.

> *We stand up against bullies.*
> *We stand up for what we believe.*
> *We are not afraid.*

WE STAND UP FOR OUR COUNTRY

A subtle symptom of the habit of fear and dread shows up in those Americans who claim they don't like their country. Often, they claim that the majority of their fellow citizens are nothing but dupes and that their government is oppressive, even murderous. Nothing their country does at home or overseas is any good. The United States of America, they say, is ruled by corporations with an intent to make money even if it hurts everyone in the world. They are so afraid of their own country that they rationalize all kinds of antisocial behavior: theft, drug-dealing, violence, even murder. Our prisons are filled with people who wouldn't be there if they just believed in their own country and the ideals represented by the Declaration of Independence and the U.S. Constitution. Unfortunately, many criminals have been taught to resent their country and their history and find themselves caught up in an awful kind of fear. Such fear and self-defeatism can only be stopped by a sound education, which includes a thorough understanding of not only what our country has done over the centuries, but why it has done it, and the principles on which it has acted. The United States has been wrong but never for the reasons the haters inside our country claim. Our ideals are good, our principles wonderful, the documents that are our foundation impeccable. The only problem with the United States is that human beings govern her, and human beings make mistakes. Only the fear mongers among us or the historically uninformed can't see that. They believe the lies and thus take on the habits of fear and dread and turn them against their own, sweet country.

The people of Coalwood had an unwavering belief in their

country, and it gave them a sense of peace. Why fear anything when your cause is just and your country good? They believed that there was no finer country in the world, not because it had a better class of people, or because it was beautiful or prosperous or even peaceful. The men and women who built Coalwood believed in their country because of what it stood for as expressed in the Declaration of Independence and the Constitution. Both were studied very closely in our schools. "We are more than just a country," Mrs. Mahoney taught in her history class. "We are a set of principles." She told us our country represented a wisdom that set us apart from most of the rest of the world. Our whole way of life was based on the belief that all humans have the right of life, liberty and the pursuit of happiness. It wasn't our government that granted us those rights, she said, but our Creator, no matter how we defined him. She went on to say that because we believed these things to be true, we'd fought the most powerful country in the world to gain our independence. Then, after we'd won it, we'd written our Constitution in such a way so as to guarantee those rights to everybody who lived in our land. She also said that when we got tired of being hypocrites, we rose up and fixed the awful institution of slavery, and more things were written in our Constitution to keep slavery from ever happening again. There were still things that were wrong in our country, she said, and there always would be. But we had written down some wonderful things, and everybody in the country was trying to follow them. The more I heard about my nation, the more I was proud of it. It made me unafraid of growing up and going out into my country. It was a good country, and I could help it maybe to be even better.

Every morning in the Coalwood School, we recited the Pledge of Allegiance to the flag. During the first few years of saying the pledge I didn't understand what it all meant, but it gradually sank in. Our flag was unique because we were unique by what we believed. The flag was a symbol of us as a people. If we ever had to fight for our country, it would be the symbol we would rally around. We learned the importance of such symbols by identifying with our mascots at school. At the Coalwood School, we were the Robins. We cheered for the Robins on the football field and the basketball court and at track meets. We were the Robins no matter where we went, and we were proud of it. At Big Creek High School we became the Owls, and we thought of ourselves as the mighty Owls, not just the athletic teams but all of us. These were the symbols that defined our schools, just as we came to understand the American flag defined all of us. The greatest difference between our school symbols and the Stars and Stripes, however, was the ideas and ideals represented by our Declaration of Independence and the Constitution. Next to the Bible, we considered these to be the holiest of documents on Earth. Reverend Richard, in his inherent wisdom, even gave a prayer about this very thing during one of Coalwood's Independence Day celebrations. He also got in a plug for education at the same time. It became a classic prayer in Coalwood. This is pretty much what he said:

> *Dear Lord, we are gathered here to celebrate not just the independence of our great land, but also the document on which it stands. There is much to admire in that document but what we best remember is this: We hold these truths to be self-evident; that all men are*

created equal; that they are endowed by their Creator with certain inalienable rights; that among these are life, liberty and the pursuit of happiness.

To prepare for this invocation today, I have pondered long and hard these words. Most of you know that I rarely go anywhere without my Bible. It is an old Bible. It belonged to my grandfather. What you don't know is that inside this book, I have always kept a copy of the Declaration of Independence. It also belonged to my grandfather. He believed it to be as holy as his Bible.

When I was a boy, somebody once asked me if my grandfather had been a slave. I couldn't imagine that could be true so I went to him and asked him: Grandfather, were you a slave? He said, Child, a man called me that, but I was never a slave, and do you know why? Because I could read. My mama, she taught me when that man wasn't looking, just as her mama taught her.

When he became officially a free man, my grandfather purchased this Bible and a copy of the Declaration of Independence. He kept them both until the day he died. He left them to me.

I have come to understand my grandfather was right. No man or woman can be a slave if they can read, especially if they can read the Bible and the American Declaration of Independence.

But that means there are still slaves in this land. There are slaves who do not know that they have inalienable rights given to them by God, and that they also have, by the grace of the Lord, life, liberty, and the right to pursue their happiness and the happiness of their families.

They are slaves to their own ignorance. Ignorance is the ultimate slaveowner.

So on this Fourth of July, I pray a special prayer.

I pray for the day when the tyranny of ignorance will be banished all across this great land and every man, woman and child can read and understand what they read.

I pray for that day.

I pray every day for that day.

Nearly every grown man in Coalwood, at one time or another, had been a soldier, sailor, marine or airman. My father, surprisingly enough, never served in the military. During World War II, the Captain asked the government for waivers so that he could keep some of his foremen down in the mine. Coal, after all, was needed for the war. Waivers were given, and the Captain issued one to Dad. Mom said Dad argued with the Captain about it, but the Captain wouldn't relent. Dad stayed home and mined coal. The work he did was dangerous, but it wasn't the same as serving in the military, even if all a man did there was work in an office. For the rest of his life, Dad felt as if he had let his country down. Maybe that was why he was always quick to hire a veteran, even one who didn't have a good work record. And maybe that was why, of all the things I did with my life, the proudest I ever made him was when I went into the army and then to Vietnam to fight for my country. I was glad to do it, for Dad as well as for myself.

Coalwood men and women fought in every one of America's twentieth-century wars and distinguished themselves in battle. These were young men and women from every section of town, New Camp, Substation, Tipple, Main, Middletown, Snakeroot, Mudhole and Frog Level. White or black, Polish or Italian, it didn't matter. They were there when their country called. Some of them were heroes, and some didn't make it back. Most were just good soldiers. When they came home, a lot of them took up their jobs in the mines as if they'd only been gone for a day. They had done their duty, that was all that mattered. They didn't ask for any special recognition, didn't care anything about any parades, didn't want any medals. For the rest of their lives, they just went around with a sense of quiet satisfaction. They had stood up for their country the best way they knew how, by serving in the armed services. Knowing that they had done their duty was a bulwark against fear for the rest of their lives.

One of the most decorated soldiers in the Vietnam War was Master Sergeant (MSG) Joe Alderman, a boy from Bartley (two mountains away from Coalwood) and a graduate of Big Creek High School. Joe married Linda Holder, who was a Caretta girl in my class at the Coalwood School and at Big Creek. While Joe was serving in the Special Forces in Vietnam, and throughout his long and distinguished army career, Linda stayed home and took care of their two children. It wasn't easy being a service wife, but Linda had the strength of the people who had raised her to keep her going. After surviving all his combat experiences, Joe came down with cancer in the prime of his life. For months, he fought it with courage and dignity, but it finally wore him down. Linda was with him during all that time. When I asked her how she managed to endure all she had, she wrote this:

When Joe left for Vietnam, I knew I had to be as strong as he was. He was in the thick of the fighting, but I thought if anybody could survive, it would be Joe. I did what I could to let him know how much I loved him. I mailed him books, Rudyard Kipling poems and the sayings of John F. Kennedy. I even mailed him a Christmas tree. I knew it was important that I give him some little piece of home not only on holidays but nearly every day.

I think it was my upbringing in Caretta that kept me strong. I always knew that I could do anything because my mother told me I could. I told my parents, "If you buy me a piano, I can play it!" I did, too.

Joe and I were a team. Beginning in 1974, we served three years establishing a new Ranger battalion. It might have said on paper that Joe was doing it but I did my part, too. While caring for our daughter, Shay, who was only three at the time, I did a hundred little things for Joe and the battalion while they were out training. I even typed out the training objectives for them. I gave birth to Patrick while Joe was in the field seven months out of nine. There were so many challenges and, of course, when Joe moved, we all moved with him. We just did what we had to do. When Joe got sick, we did what we had to do then, too. It was the way we were brought up. You take the bad with the good and keep going.

These days, I live near Fort Bragg where Joe worked until he died. I hear the planes and my windows shake from artillery noises, and I pray for those who serve now, and their spouses and children, and for all those who suffered most on September 11. Ironically, Joe's birthday was September 11. He would have hated to think that this awful thing happened on his day, but then he would have heard the call and gone to war for his country. I loved him for a lot of reasons, but one reason was because he always answered the call of his country. He lived a life of service to our nation. I am not sad for the way I lived my life or for the way Joe lived his. This was the way we were raised, knowing that serving our country was the right thing to do.

To go through life without serving your country in some way is to risk looking back and wondering if perhaps you were selfish, that what you have is undeserved. When you sit in the warm comfort of your living room and watch on television the brave men and women out fighting to keep our country safe, you should not only be thankful for what they're doing but also determined to help in whatever way you can. If you're a young and healthy person, I strongly urge you to go into one of the military services. It will be good for you and good for your country. We need citizens who know what military service is and can bring back that information to friends and family. That is part of citizenship. Giving up time and sweat and sometimes blood is also a way to help pay for the freedom you enjoy. Military service is simply good for you. You will be with people who will be your friends for life. You will learn how to be a part of a team. You will have adventures and learn new skills. A few short years of service will enhance your life for all your days. If, for some reason, you can't serve in the military, there are alternatives, including volunteering in a hundred different federal, state and local organizations that will let you work for your country. I am a proud veteran so trust me on this one. If you serve your country, you will never regret it. It will help make you psychologically and physically strong. You will have a sense of accomplishment that will work like armor against fear and dread for the rest of your life.

> *We stand up for our country.*
> *We stand up for what we believe.*
> *We are not afraid.*

OTHER VOICES: WE STAND UP FOR WHAT WE BELIEVE

A Life of Service
Kathryn Bryson Davis

My father, George W. Bryson, was county superintendent of McDowell County Schools for thirty-three years. Dad was born and raised on a farm in Raleigh County, West Virginia. He attended a one-room school for eight years and went two years to a nearby high school (which at that time ended with the tenth grade). He then went to Concord College in Athens, West Virginia, where he completed the remaining two years of high school and pursued his Standard Normal Degree all at the same time, receiving it in 1921 at the age of nineteen.

From his humble beginnings, my dad went on to accomplish much in the field of education, not only for McDowell County, but also for the state of West Virginia. In 1931, he became the principal of the new consolidated high school

called Big Creek High School. In early 1935, he was
approached by a group of prominent county citizens and
asked to become the next county superintendent of schools.
He accepted and was approved by the state board. On July
1, 1935, my father assumed the office of county superintendent. I was born that same day. During all the days I knew
him, my father stood up and fought for what he believed,
and most of all, he believed it was his duty to see to the education of every child in McDowell County.

My father was reappointed as county superintendent for six
five-year terms, retiring on June 30, 1968. During all those
years his one continuing theme was to build the best school
system in the state. The effects of the Depression played a
major part in the challenge he faced. Many young men went
to school in the daytime and worked in the coal mines at night
to help support the family. Many families went without food.
Still, everybody knew the value of an education and looked to
my father to provide it for their children. Not only did Dad
keep his school system well organized and properly funded,
he paid attention to what was going on in the classrooms, too,
often visiting the schools and sitting in the back of the classes,
watching how a teacher worked and making notes on what she
needed. He took an interest in individual students, too, working hard to get them scholarships or alternative funding for
college. He believed students should have the right to pursue
their education as far as their abilities would allow. Dad hired
the best teachers he could find and fought hard to provide
some of the top salaries for teachers in the state.

My father was truly the driving force behind the McDowell
County School System, which, despite its location deep in the
hills of West Virginia, would prove to be one of the best in the

country. This is demonstrated by the great success of the students who went through his system. He was never afraid to confront any problem or person as long as it would benefit the students and teachers in McDowell County.

Fired for My Own Good
Bill Todd

My three years in high school were a great experience. I had many friends, played basketball and was a member of the famous Big Creek Owls marching band. As I entered my senior year, many of my senior classmates were making plans to attend college, but I didn't know what I was going to do. In late winter of 1955, Mr. Doyle Eskew, the art teacher at Big Creek High School, began encouraging me to attend college on the merits of my basketball ability. He arranged for me to visit the campus of West Virginia Wesleyan College at Buckhannon. After an interview with the basketball coach, I was offered a grant-in-aid. I made the traveling squad as a first-year freshman. I played and believe I would have been an asset to the team had I continued as a student at Wesleyan, but that was not to be. My grant was small, and Wesleyan was an expensive private school. I decided to come home, apply for a job with the coal company and put my college on hold indefinitely.

I interviewed for a job with Mr. Devotie Dantzler in June 1956 and got a job working for him in the company store and the service station. My first day on the job, Mr. Dantzler told me he expected me to return to college. I told him that was my intention, but I continued to work for the company through the summer of 1959. During those three years, Mr. Dantzler would often ask about my plans to return to school. I would always say I was thinking about it when really I was not giving it any thought at all. I was enjoying making a little money. In May 1959, I was ordered to come to his office. Being called to the office was not a matter taken lightly. It often meant that you were in trouble over a work-related issue. Mr. Dantzler asked me to come in and sit down. He explained that he had never fired an employee for not going to college but that in my case he was going to make an exception. He said I had until the end of August, but that would be the last day I would ever work for him. I had no choice. I went back to college. I had been fired for my own good.

I continue to be impressed by the generation of people like my parents and Mr. Dantzler. They were hard-working, honest, reliable, friendly and helpful people. I reflect often on the neighbors who lived in the row of coal company houses where I grew up. The corner home of Homer and Elsie Hickam, Cecil and Rosemary Sharitz, my parents Ray and Ada Todd, Ted and Naomi Keneda, Charles and Fanny McGlothlin, and at the end of our row the home of two of my favorite relatives, Uncle Chris and Aunt Dent Todd. It was my good fortune to have these wonderful people as role models. Their dedication to God, job, family and neighbors shaped my values and my life.

I graduated from Marshall University in 1962, married in 1963 and have three children, all of whom also attended college. I recently retired from a satisfying and rewarding management career in manufacturing. Although he's passed on now, nearly every day I still thank Mr. Dantzler for firing me for my own good.

A Coal Miner's Determination
Fred K. Bailey

My father died when I was seven years old, and my mother married John K. Morrison when I was eight or nine. My stepfather was a coal miner at Island Creek Coal Company at the Bartley #1 Mine, a couple of mountains away from Coalwood. He began his career as a union man and later in his working years rose to the position of section foreman. Mr. Morrison had eight children when he and my mother were married. He was a part-time minister in the Baptist church and traveled throughout McDowell County evangelizing. I'm sure he realized his lack of formal education was a detriment to his career as he only completed the second grade. I can vividly remember him asking me to bring a chair to sit beside him at his desk on many cold winter nights. I was in the sixth grade at the time, and he asked me to teach him math and English. We started at the front of the books and worked our way through. As I sat beside him, he never hesitated to ask questions or request help. He was a great student because his motivation was to better himself in whatever way he could. I'm very proud that he chose me to be his tutor. He worked in the mines for over forty years, and he believed in the value of education. I'm sure that his desire for education was a motivating factor for me to obtain my bachelor's and master's degrees. I eventually became principal of Big Creek High School. Mr. Morrison was truly a determined person, and I am a better man today because of his influence.

More Than a Common Laborer
Bill Hardin

When I grew up in Coalwood, my dad was the maintenance chief for the coal mine. He had been an electrician, and I think a mechanic before that. My birth certificate lists his occupation as "common laborer," but he was driven to be more. Dad studied every night and every weekend. As long as I can remember, and even after I left home, his home life was the black mine phone and the books and schematics for all the mine equipment (which I still have). He was very successful; he had designs of his own incorporated by Westinghouse and a bunch of other manufacturers. The electric brake used by the coal company on its trams was one of his ideas. But the lack of a college degree was like a lead weight to him. He didn't talk to his son much, but hell or high water, I knew at an early age I would be going to college. I went to college, and even though I didn't end up getting a degree, I advanced to high corporate positions and had Ph.D.'s working for me before I was thirty years old.

I used to love when Dad would take me on his inspection runs on weekends. He didn't take me too often, but it was like we were the only people in that vast mine. I don't think people can comprehend the size of the mine until they've toured it on a puddle jumper. He'd talk to me on those days, tell me stories about what was going on, miner's gossip. We'd go check all the pumps, rectifiers and whatever else. I was fascinated with the motor barn, close to the shaft. His office was there, desk, file cabinets, even a flush-up john. It was his place, and he loved it.

I never fully understood what held men like my dad to

that mine. He started to work for the company on his birth-day at Big Creek High School graduation in May 1939 and was still working for them when he died on his birthday thirty-five years later to the day. Several years before, I took him for a test ride in my new Oldsmobile, and he told me he had been offered a job as a federal mine inspector. If he took the job, he could stay in Coalwood as home base. It was a wonderful offer. He had enough years to retire from Olga Coal, and the mine inspector's job had to be a fairly high GS-level job, with good benefits and a federal retirement pro-gram. But my dad would not consider leaving the company. He started there, and he would finish there. It was part of who he was, the kind of man who always stood up for what he believed, and he believed in Coalwood and supported the company that had built it.

WE STAND UP FOR WHAT WE BELIEVE: A SUMMARY

The people of Coalwood were not much prone to showing weakness. They had the sense to know that to show weakness was the same as showing fear and letting dread rule their lives. Accordingly, they adopted the attitude of standing up for what they believed, even though they might, in the end, lose their argument. They didn't believe in vio-lence with this attitude, but they did believe that if a thing was worth believing, it was worth arguing and fighting for, too. I've named a few of the things that Coalwoodians stood up for: themselves, each other, tough teachers, honest men, their country and against bullies. But these weren't the only things they were willing to fight for. The list was endless because it varied from citizen to citizen. But when men or women stood up for whatever was important to them, they were allowed to have their say. Coalwood people were always respectful and willing to listen even though they might disagree in the end.

If you acquire the attitude of standing up for what you believe, it will help you stop being afraid. This does not mean that every time you feel you're being slighted, you should erupt with loud, hateful behavior. Standing up for what you believe has nothing to do with being violent or being obnoxious because of some perceived oppression. This attitude has to do with a quiet determination to have your opinion explained and heard. To be effective, it also has to be respectful and fair. Yelling and cursing isn't standing up for what you believe. It's simply being arrogant and foolish. The most effective way of standing up is always going to be the nonviolent way, quiet but determined. Gandhi and Martin Luther King Jr. proved that. There are times, however, when our country has to go to war to defend our citizens against those who know only violence. When those times come, we need to stand up for our country and fight.

The habits of fear and dread may make you want to hide and to deliberately appear weak in the hope that others will just leave you alone because you aren't worth opposing. To take on this attitude of weakness will, given time, strip you of your self-respect, separate you from the rest of your community and leave you only a shell of a person, cowering in anonymity. The best way to break free of this attitude is to become truly informed so that your opinions are based on facts. It's hard work, having an opinion that you can defend, but it's worth it. You'll be willing to stand up for something you've put out a little sweat to conclude. Once you start standing up—and, again, this always needs to be done respectfully—you'll find that you are stronger than perhaps you thought you were. That's what the people of Coalwood knew and why they urged everyone, no matter who they were, to express their opinion and fight for whatever they believed.

> *We stand up for what we believe.*
> *We are not afraid.*

Coalwood Attitude

#3

We keep our families together.

Reminder: It is not the purpose of this book to tell you what is moral. For that, I suggest a visit to your local preacher, priest or rabbi. If I tried to start preaching, the people who raised me would no doubt accuse me of being puffed up. They'd say, and rightly so, that if I wanted to be a preacher, then I should first learn how to live out of a collection plate. The people of Coalwood could never abide a preacher who had a dime in his pocket. Fortunately for me, the idea behind this book is not to preach but to recall how the people of Coalwood managed to live good and happy lives even though they always lived in the perilous times of the mid-twentieth century West Virginia coalfields. By recalling the attitudes of the people who raised me, it is my intention that others might have a model for their own lives, one that will help them avoid the habits of fear and dread. Of course, if morality and goodness are revealed in my stories of Coalwood, I hope the people who raised me will forgive me for nearly preaching. After all, it isn't my fault that they lived the fine lives they did.

The company men who ran Coalwood thought they had a firm grip on how their town should be run and what was needed to keep things going. They believed that for the town to be strong, the families that lived there had to be strong, too. Accordingly, they designed and built the town to support families. For family recreation, they constructed baseball fields around town, built several parks with playground equipment and constructed the Coalwood Conservation Club (also known as "The Cabin") on top of a nearby mountain. They supported and funded active Boy Scout, Girl Scout, Cub Scout and Brownie troops. When they built a new school, they converted the old one into a community building where the Scouts and other clubs could meet. The basement of the community building was a big, open room that was used for birthday parties and dances for kids and adults alike. For a long time, the company had a movie theater. When attendance dropped, the theater was torn down and tennis courts built on the same spot. Soon, many of Coalwood's children were expert tennis players and were going off to compete in upstate tournaments, attended by proud Coalwood parents.

To further enhance the community and the families within, the company sponsored a "Home of the Month" contest, and competition was fierce. Splashes of color from rose gardens and petunia plots were in nearly every yard. Grass was carefully cultivated and always kept mown. More than once, I spied a big, tough miner down on his hands and knees with a pair of yard shears, delicately paring a corner of turf that lined his pansy beds. If a yard got the least bit messy, the gossip-fence rattled with displeasure until the miscreants got the message. Houses were scrubbed annually to peel off the coal dirt that tended to build up from the passing coal trains. The company kept painters busy year-round, continuously going from house to house to put on fresh coats of pure white paint. When the *Washington Post* sent a reporter down to write about the expected abysmal conditions of McDowell County coal camps, he ended up writing about a charming little "Alpine village" named Coalwood.

Coalwood's churches were kept immaculate so that families might worship in a decent place. The preachers were considered company men, and their requests for mainte-nance and repairs were always heeded. On Wednesday nights and Sunday mornings, the church bells rang and the choirs sang and the whole town seemed to swell in joyful praise of the Lord. Coalwood's life was essentially an industrial sym-phony, its churches and playgrounds and the surrounding mountains and the mine all blending to make a kind of music that you could almost hear. The seasons changed, from bright, crisp falls, through deep, snowy winters, to lively, buoyant springs that changed into hot, lazy summers, but the town was always a constant hum of activity, each citizen going about their lives, knowing who they were and why they existed and what they needed to do. And one of the most important things they always needed to do, the people of Coalwood believed, was to keep their families together.

Coalwood's position on the family was clear: A family was an absolute obligation as well as a great source of strength. To allow a family to break apart was an alien concept. A man who lost his family, especially if it was through his own inat-tention or maybe from fooling around with the painted women at Cinder Bottom three mountains away, was considered a sorry soul in Coalwood. The company wanted no part of him because he had proved that he couldn't be entirely trusted. His parents and grandparents and friends hardly knew what to do with such a man, either. Obviously, he had failed at the most important thing in the world, being a husband and a father. A few men tried to hang on in town after a divorce, but it never worked out. Soon, they were gone, to where it was not known or much cared.

These days, some people have taken the attitude that keeping a family together isn't necessary for a happy life. How, they say, can the kids be happy if the parents aren't happy with one another? Better by far to give up on a marriage and go after that better-looking, more understanding potential spouse rather than stay in an unhappy marriage. Coalwood's people never bought into that kind of thinking for the simple reason they believed, and experience had shown them, that the most joy in life can be gained by building a family and keeping it together. They knew there were various stages of a person's life, and that impetuous youth gave way eventually to a more solid-thinking age. Husbands and wives fought, but they always remembered they were family and they weren't going to go anywhere except eventually back into each other's arms. It was an attitude that made them strong and unafraid, because the outcome was certain no matter how bitter the argument. In the end, they would find a way to stay together.

Coalwood's concept of the family was clear. A family meant one set of parents and kids, forever intact. The importance of having only intact families in Coalwood was a serious matter. Anything less was seen as a threat to the town's integrity, not to mention a bad example for everyone, especially for young people. It was expected that the adults in a family would act like adults and therefore do their duty to the family they had created, and hold it close until the day they died. About the only wavering in this attitude was when a husband or wife took to beating up each other or the kids, or had proved to be unfaithful and unrepentant at the same time. Coalwood recognized some people had to be banished from the family for everybody's good. Still, the basic attitude was that once you produced a family, it was your responsibility to keep it going. It was one of the fundamental reasons Coalwood people were able to beat fear and avoid dread. They believed that as long as you had your family, you had everything you needed for a good life, and it gave them continuous reassurance that all was well.

When I grew up in Coalwood I only knew one child whose parents were divorced, and I always felt sorry for him. He wasn't a Coalwood boy. He just came to town every so often to visit his grandparents. It seemed to me the boy was always a little scared, and I could see why. From my perspective, his life was unbelievably complicated. His father had a wife who wasn't his mother. His mother had a husband who wasn't his father. He didn't have one house. He had two that he was supposed to think of as home, although not at the same time. All the Coalwood kids I knew were secure in who they were and where they lived and who their parents were. It was all so simple, even I could figure it out. But I don't think that boy was ever sure about much of anything. He ended up in reform school, or so I heard. At least he knew where his home was while he was there. It was probably a comfort.

The concept of what a family is has been a matter of some debate in recent years. Some people say a family is whatever they decide it should be. That was definitely not the way the people of Coalwood saw it. As far as they were concerned, the family should be kept as simple as possible. The father was the titular head of the family, a source of manly strength and authority. The mother actually ran things in the household day-to-day and was the true authority for what went on under her roof. Every child, according to the sequence in which they were born, had their own place in the family as they matured. Older kids had the most responsibility and on down the line. It wasn't complicated, and it kept everybody in the family secure because everybody knew where they fit. As a former NASA engineer, I learned that any time a mechanism gets too complex, it starts to have more opportunities to fail. That's why rockets blow up. Rockets are actually simple machines, but the more demands that are made on them—to fly faster, soar higher, to separate as stages, to carry payloads and so forth—required us engineers to design them to be more complex. The possibilities of failure increased with each complication. Families are like that, too. When the organizational lines within them go up and down and sideways, when traditional roles are all mixed up, when it isn't clear as to where everybody fits, it's inevitable that families gets confused, and there's nothing like confusion to breed fear.

From my long observation of people, I've come to believe we're genetically hard-wired to be part of a specific kind of family. It's true of every other kind of mammal on this planet, so why should we think we're any different? Lions organize themselves into prides and wolves into packs and nearly every other mammal on Earth has a group they associate with, but they're all just families according to their genetic dispositions. Some are patriarchal, some matriarchal, but all follow the same pattern based on what kind of mammal they are. I can't imagine that this isn't true for us human kind of mammals, too. When we become part of a family organization that isn't recognized by our particular genetic mammalian disposition, it results in stress. It's worse for human children. A mom here, a father over there, being shunted from pillar to post, all are corrosive to a sense of order, and there's nobody who craves order more than a human child. A child's world just isn't right when the family gets too complicated. This was something the people of Coalwood knew instinctively, so they did their best to keep things simple.

Families were nurtured in Coalwood. The entire community was set up to support the family. A single miner had to live in a boarding house or the Club House. He got a bare room with a narrow bed, a table, a couple of hard-backed chairs and a communal bathroom down the hall. Sometimes, his bed wasn't even his own. When he rolled out of it to go to work, another miner coming off-shift often rolled in. He ate at a long table, competing with the other single men for the food served up in big bowls and massive platters. Forks stabbed wildly and spoons were flailed about. If a man wasn't fast, he might not get much to eat. Except for an occasional card game with the other single miners, it was a lonely existence. But when a miner got married, everything changed and for the better. The young couple got a house with indoor plumbing, a fully equipped kitchen and at least two bedrooms, one for them, the other for the children soon to come. Promotion at work became more likely. Married men were trusted more than single fellows. They were thought of as vastly more serious-minded. At the union hall, the voice of the husband and father carried much more weight than the single lad's. Being single was thought of as an interim state, a temporary condition, one that should be dispensed with upon maturity. Single people were thought of as not quite complete. Married couples were the norm. And children without properly married fathers and mothers were simply not known. The churches in town, white and black, would have thundered against such impropriety. No child was going to be raised in Coalwood outside a family. If it took a shotgun to make that happen, then most every daughter's father in town knew where his was, and it was kept well oiled. Young men and women got together, courted, married and had babies, in that order, creating something miraculous—a family. It was life according to tradition, solid and everlasting, life as it was meant to be, as all the generations before them had lived. There was a comfort to that and, ultimately, the kind of fulfillment you can only receive when you've lived the right way and know it.

Unfortunately, according to the statistics I've seen, there is a strong possibility that the reader of this book did not grow up in what Coalwood people thought of as an intact family. And there's also a possibility that you are an adult who has let your family come apart. Both situations probably have made you unhappy, and whether you've thought of it this way or not, it's also made you afraid, too. And once you become fearful of one aspect of your life, it becomes all the more likely that fear will take over in other ways, too.

If you are a husband or wife who has allowed your family to fall apart, the people of Coalwood would surely urge you to put it back together again. And if you're certain it's too late to put your family back as it was, they would say you should at least try to repair the damage. Let your children know that you appreciate and understand their confusion and make certain they know exactly where they fit, even if everybody doesn't live together. That's the best way to help your children feel secure. Do the best you can do, that's all I can tell you. But if you already have an intact family, resolve from here to infinity to keep it that way. It will be a courageous and powerful thing to do, and it will make you all the more brave and strong to do it.

We keep our families together.
We are not afraid.

We Make Our Families Sacred

It was a big event in Coalwood when a man finally settled down and got married. This was true whether the man came out of Snakeroot or New Camp or any other part of town. The color of the man or his position at the mine had no bearing on his marriage. What mattered was that it got done, and properly so. But sometimes, even after a marriage and a family was created, things didn't work out according to the Coalwood way. When that happened, the result was usually hardship for everybody in town. One man who caused such hardship lived up in Mudhole. I shall call him Chester.

Chester grew up in Mudhole. He was a star football player at Excelsior High School and graduated with top honors. When he entered the army, it was just in time for the Korean War. In Korea, he gave a good account of himself, driving a supply truck up and down through the combat zones. He received a couple of medals, which he proudly sent home to his folks. Of course, they took them to the Big Store to show them off. My mom told Dad at the kitchen table about seeing Chester's medals and said that she hoped the young man would come back to Coalwood. Dad gave it some thought, then said, "The next time you see Chester's mom, tell her Chester's got a job at the mine any time he wants it."

Dad was as good as his word, and when Chester came home and applied for work, he got it. He was assigned to work with the rock dust crew on the hoot-owl shift. He was a good worker, and he was also known to be a good softball player, an important attribute at a time when all the coal companies had softball teams. Before long, Chester was one of Coalwood's best players. Everybody admired him. Chester lived at home with his folks and showed up every Sunday morning at the Reverend Richard's Mudhole Church of Distinct Christianity to worship. Then he pleased everybody in town when he came home from a softball game saying he had found a girl in Bradshaw he was going to marry. Her name was Rachel.

Rachel turned out to be a very nice young lady, although she came from a rough background. Her father had left her family when she was just a baby. Her mother had done her best with nine children, but eventually all the kids had been farmed out around the Negro community in Bradshaw. Rachel had gotten little formal education, but she was a hard worker and kept her house spotless. As far as Coalwood's women were concerned, Rachel was a good addition to the community, and she was accepted just as if she had been born and raised there. Soon, Chester and Rachel had themselves a fine baby daughter who they named Chesra, after themselves.

Two houses below John Eye's Moonshine Emporium up

in Snakeroot lived a girl named Emma. Emma was a source of great disappointment to her parents. She dropped out of school and worked for awhile over in Cinder Bottom as an easy lady. Two years after Chesra was born, Chester and Emma began to slip around and see each other. Chester's team members on the rock dust crew figured it out first. Something that Chester said started them wondering, and after awhile he confessed it to them. "I love her, fellows," Chester said. "Emma makes me so happy I could bust."

His rock dust boss said, "You have a wife, Chester. You picked her and you got married in the church. And the two of you begot Chesra. This ain't right, what you're doing with Emma. It could tear your family to pieces."

But Chester shrugged. "Emma makes me happy" was his reply.

"Not everything makes you happy now is going to make you happy forever, Chester," the rock dust boss told him.

It didn't take long, of course, before Rachel found out about her husband and Emma. When Chester came home from work one day, he found all his clothes pitched in the front yard. When Chester tried to go home to his parents, they wouldn't hear of it. They told him he had wronged Rachel and should go home and beg her forgiveness. Petulantly, he rented himself a little shack over on Premier Mountain. Emma got kicked out of her parents' house, too, and pretty soon moved into the little Premier shack. This put the coal company in a hard place. Rachel and Chesra were living in company housing. Without Chester, according to the company rules, Rachel and Chesra would have to leave. A delegation of Snakeroot and Mudhole men went to my dad to convince him to give Rachel more time. Dad agreed and also saw to it that Chester's pay was garnisheed to keep paying the rent, but that was all he could do. Chester was in the union, and under the union contract, a man could only be fired for a work-related cause. Being an unfaithful husband and a poor father wasn't described in the contract even though his fellow union members didn't like what Chester had done, either. Chester kept his job, although he found himself isolated at work. He didn't seem to care. "Emma makes me happy" was all that Chester would say over and over again when the other men on his crew worried about his family in Mudhole. Everybody was disgusted with Chester but confident that disaster would seek him out, which it did, but as often happens, it was first visited on the innocent. God has his ways, as the people of Coalwood so often said, and they are not ours.

To get by, Rachel had to take work. Although the rent was handled, Chester didn't provide any money for food or the little things a baby needed. Emma took all the money he brought home. She liked fancy things like velvet shoes with rhinestones on their toes. Rachel got a job as a maid to a rich woman in Welch. Every day, she drove across Welch Mountain to take care of one of the big houses on the hill that overlooked the county seat. Chesra was left with a neighbor lady. One day, while crawling around the neighbor's kitchen, she somehow managed to turn over a hot pot of soup on top of herself. Her screams brought the neighbor, who raced the little girl to the company doctor. The doctor did what he could, then drove the scalded little girl over to the emergency hospital in Welch. Rachel met them there. Chesra was in terrible pain but it appeared she might live, although with terrible scars.

When Chester heard about what had happened, he rushed to the hospital but was blocked by his own mother. "But I'm Chesra's father!" he protested. "No, Chester," his mother told him. "You're the man what got her mother pregnant, that's all. Now get your sorry self out of here!"

Chester went with his head hung low to the Reverend Richard, who told him that God forgave but Coalwood didn't. He'd provide him a few proverbs if he wanted, but that wasn't about to solve his problem. "What you got to do, Chester, is to figure out something. That something is what kind of a man you are."

"I'm a good man," Chester said defensively. "I work hard, and I make good money."

"That ain't what I mean and you know it," the Reverend replied, but he left it at that. Some things, the Reverend would later tell folks, a man has to figure out for himself or it doesn't work half as good.

When Chester went to their shack on Premier Mountain, Emma was there, but even though she was still the same Emma and nothing had changed about her, Chester knew everything had changed about himself, but he wasn't sure exactly what. It wasn't too long before Emma left him, saying, "You're no fun anymore." She headed for Washington, D.C., where she could maybe find a rich man to take care of her. Chester was left alone in his shack. *I'm a good man,* he kept telling himself. *I just wanted to be happy.*

In the next few months, Chester seemed to age rapidly. He took on a slow gait and kept his head hanging. He went into the mine and rode the man-trip into work every day and did his job, but he did it without enthusiasm. Every so often, he'd sneak into Mudhole at night and watch Rachel and

Chesra through the lighted windows. Most of Chesra's scars were down her back and legs, but there was a horrible patch on her face, too, that encompassed one ear. Chester knew her scars was his fault, and he mourned over it. Every day, it seemed he felt a little sadder. Most days, he wished he wouldn't wake up, but when he did, he had to face the reality of what he had caused.

After awhile, another man who lived in Mudhole, a widower, came courting Rachel. He was two decades older but he was gentle and good, and Chesra liked him. Rachel sent Chester a note through his coworkers that she wanted a divorce so she could marry her widower. After reading it, Chester came undone. He simply collapsed. He had to be carried from the mine where he was unceremoniously dumped in front of the bathhouse. If he expected sympathy, he didn't get any. His fellow miners knew he'd brought his problems on himself. Men stepped over him to get to the showers. After awhile, he got up and walked down the hill to his car. He drove to Mudhole, determined to see Rachel and Chesra. Rachel met him at the door and listened to him while he sobbed out all of his regret and remorse. "I know I've done wrong," he said at the end. "I want to come home."

Rachel told him to sit down on the porch swing, then she went down and told his mother what had happened. His mother called the Reverend Richard, who called other people. At least two dozen people came and sat on the porch, including the widower who was in love with Rachel. Reverend Richard took charge. "I married these two," he said. "They promised themselves to one another. They have a duty to themselves and to little Chesra to stay together."

"But he cheated on Rachel," the widower argued. "He

hurt her bad. And because he made her have to work, little Chesra got herself burned."

Everybody on the porch agreed that was so. "But these three are a family," the Reverend said. "If they can patch themselves up, they got to do it. A family is a duty once it's taken on. Even more than that. It's a sacred thing."

Chester said he agreed with all that and Rachel, after a little prodding, said she did, too. "I don't love you no more, Chester," she said, looking him straight in the eye. "But you can come home if you don't mind living with a woman who don't respect you and won't ever show you any feeling. You make sure you understand. I ain't ever gonna love you again, not even hug you, don't matter what you do. But little Chesra, she needs her father. That's all I'm saying."

Chester dropped his head, but after a little while the Reverend raised his face up with a hand under his chin. "You listen to me, Chester," he said. "By what you've done, you've made yourself weak. You shuffle around like some decrepit old man. Your face is all crumbly. That is just part of the wages you've earned for losing your family." The Reverend turned Chester's head to where Rachel held Chesra. The little girl smiled shyly through her scars at her father. "There is your strength. It was always there. But you gave up strength just to be happy in a frivolous way. Everybody knows it's work to keep a family. But in the end, it will give out happiness like none other. It's just the way of this old world."

The widower, hearing all this, could not help but agree. "I took care of my wife until the day she died," he declared. "I wouldn't like myself much if I hadn't done what was right."

Rachel and Chesra went inside and everybody left, leaving Chester alone on the porch to sort the last few things out.

After awhile, he got up, wiped his hands on his britches, his eyes with the back of his sleeve, and went inside. Whatever passed between him and Rachel after that was not known. Neither would talk of it, but it was noticed Rachel never showed Chester any affection in public. Still, Chester seemed to find his strength again. Two years after he got his family back, he took his foreman's test and became one of West Virginia's first black mine supervisors. Chesra grew up into a fine young woman and went to Bluefield State College and graduated as a nurse. After a career in the mine, Chester died of black lung. As he lay in the hospital bed breathing his last labored breaths, Rachel got up from her chair and sat down on the edge of the bed and took him in her arms. It was said of Chester when he died that there was no happier man in Coalwood.

> *We make our families sacred.*
> *We keep our families together.*
> *We are not afraid.*

WE DON'T FORGET OUR REAL JOB

Every man in Coalwood knew that his real job, the most important one he would ever have, was to keep his family together. That meant staying alive in the coal mine because the Coalwood Proposition had a corollary that said if you got yourself killed, your family would have to leave within two weeks. It was not a corollary that anybody much admired, but it was accepted as necessary. The house occupied by the widow and her kids was needed by the new miner and his family coming in. Just knowing that his family would lose their home was enough to keep most miners careful and safe in the mine. One time, my father forgot what his real job was and put himself in a risky position. That was when my mother had to take the time to explain to him an important thing about his family, something he should have already known.

It started with an accident. Slate had come loose on a section and tore past the roof bolts. A piece with an edge like a razor decapitated a man, but that wasn't the end of it. The slate continued to fall until it had trapped all the miners on the section, and there they stayed with the poor man's body and his head until my dad led a rescue party in, ripping his hands bloody pulling the slate out of the tunnel. It was a close-run thing. The trapped men very nearly ran out of air. As it was, some of them had turned nearly blue from the cold and stale atmosphere.

Dad came out of the mine that day with an idea. What if there was always a way to get out no matter where you were in the mine? The coal company used huge fans, strategically placed to blow air down shafts from the surface into the mine. There were also smaller shafts to provide incidental ventilation. What if they could be used for escape?

Dad's plan was simple. Dot the mine with shafts and use steel casings as emergency man-lifts to the surface. In 1953, he convinced the general superintendent that this was a good idea and began a two-year campaign to make it happen. The shafts were to be thirty-inches wide and drilled seven hundred feet through solid rock. Dad did the engineering himself, solving pressure problems, inventing new drilling techniques, devising methods of lining the hole with concrete as the drilling proceeded so as to seal the shafts from shifting rock and the unimaginable pressure of deep underground lakes. He drove his men to drill, to dig and to build the man-lifts. During the last month before the first shaft punched through into the air space of a tunnel, he forgot at times even to come home. He was obsessed with his idea.

When the shafts were complete, only one thing remained to do. They needed to be tested. Dad had designed the man-lift to be a fourteen-foot torpedo-shaped cylinder. There were two large openings in it, one directly above the other. Between the openings was a steel floor. Each compartment would hold two men in a tight squeeze. A mobile crane was brought to one of the shafts to lift a cylinder into place for a test. A large gathering of men was there to witness it, state and federal safety men, foremen of the mine, the doctor and the dentist, my dad, and Mr. Van Dyke, Dad's boss. Four men had volunteered to ride the cylinder during the test, but once they saw the reality of what they were supposed to do, they decided maybe they didn't want to do it after all. Seven hundred feet was a long way to ride down a narrow tube wedged inside a steel casement suspended from a long, thin cable. There was much foot shuffling until Dad walked up on the platform and stepped inside his invention. In a show of confidence, Mr. Van Dyke climbed inside the other compartment and the cylinder was lowered. Halfway down Mr. Van Dyke leaned back against the cylinder and it swung minutely and wedged itself in the shaft. The cylinder stopped, completely stuck.

On the surface, the men noticed that the cable didn't look right. A call to the men at the bottom of the shaft confirmed that the torpedo hadn't made it all the way. Everybody stood in shocked silence until the crane operator got an idea. The company had an old fire truck, once used to dampen down the coal dust around the tipple. Maybe it could be used to dump water down the shaft and lubricate the torpedo. By the time the fire truck arrived, the rescue torpedo had been stuck in the shaft for almost an hour. A deluge of water fell down the black hole while the operator carefully pulled the cable back. With the water making the sides slippery, the torpedo broke free, and in ten minutes my dad and Mr. Van Dyke were back on the surface, wet but alive.

Dad wasn't willing to give up. Although Mr. Van Dyke headed for home, my father got back into the cylinder and ordered it dropped again. He stood very precisely at the center of the cylinder, and this time it went all the way down to the bottom where he stepped off, turned around and rode it back up again. No one ever rode the torpedo man-lift again, but Dad had at least proved his point that it could be done.

It didn't take long, house-by-house, fence-by-fence, for my mom to hear what had happened. A lot of people were praising Dad as a hero. I was in the dining room, heading for the kitchen, when I heard his footsteps wearily coming up the steps from the basement. Mom swung open the basement door and something told me to stop where I was.

Mom seemed to fall down the basement steps at least once a year and had the bruises to show for it. I don't know if this time she slipped or did it deliberately, but the whole house shook as the two of them tumbled head over heels to the bottom of the steps. I ran to the basement door. Mom had pulled herself up and she had grabbed Dad by his shirt. She hissed into his face, "Don't you ever, ever, *ever* do anything like that again or, I swear, I'll take the boys and you'll never see us again!"

Dad tried to rise and then fell back. "It's my job," he said, rubbing the back of his head where it had hit the steps.

She pointed up to where I stood frozen in place by fear and fascination. "*There's* your job," she snapped. "Your *family's* your job." She put her face in her hands. "*I'm* your job."

I saw him put a tentative hand on her cheek and wipe clumsily at her tears. The next morning, Dad went to work before dawn, but he came home earlier than usual that day. And for the next few days, I saw him home while the sun was still up. That was quite a marvel. I guess he'd remembered where his real job was.

> *We don't forget our real job.*
> *We keep our families together.*
> *We are not afraid.*

WE LOVE OUR ANIMALS

Sometimes fear expresses itself through cruelty, usually against some poor creature that can't defend itself. I recall a time when I was at a party and the man who was hosting it told a story about catching a cat when he lived in New York City, soaking it with water, then throwing it outside on a snowy night to freeze to death. He told his story, laughing the entire time as if his story was the funniest thing in the world. The response from his audience was stunned silence, then everybody edged away from him. I could never see that man afterwards without feeling contempt for him. Of all the manifestations of being afraid, the worst is to get joy from hurting animals. Every child in Coalwood was brought up to respect animals, and if one was brought into our homes as a pet, they became part of the family and given the love and attention they deserved.

Loving animals was a tradition in Coalwood that went all the way back to both Mr. Carters, the older and younger. When the first Mr. Carter opened his mine, he employed teams of mules to haul out the coal. He saw to it that they had a first-class mule barn and that no mule stayed too long down in the mine. He had enough of them that they could be rotated in and out, and he insisted that the teamsters not use whips. If a mule got sick, he sent the town doctor to treat it. If one broke its leg, it was dispatched quickly lest it feel too much pain. This respect for the working mules of Coalwood was passed on to the younger Mr. Carter when his father died. When the Coalwood mine started using electric locomotives to carry out the coal, the mules were retired but were kept at the mule barn. The field in front of the Mudhole Church was their pasture, and there were strict orders that the mules were not to be played with by the town boys, neither ridden nor heckled in any way. The people of Coalwood came to love their mules, but when President Truman sent in the navy to occupy Coalwood and bring in the union, Mr. Carter was forced to sell out, lock, stock, barrel and mules. One of the first things the new company did was to sell the mules to the glue factories and renderers. The women of Coalwood, tears streaming down their cheeks, lined the street as their mules were carted out of town on open trucks. They were showing their respect for the animals that had not only helped to build Coalwood but had become family. Many people in our little town never forgave the new company for what they did to our mules.

In the Hickam household, there were always pets. My mom loved all kinds of animals. When she was first married, somebody in Florida mailed her a baby alligator for a wedding gift. She named it Albert and raised it in the bathtub until it got too big and chased my future father down the steps. Reluctantly, she agreed to let it go but insisted Dad drive her to Florida to release it in a warm river. Dad had to take almost a week off from work to get her and Albert all the way to Florida, but he did it, driving night and day to get there, then wandering all over the swamplands until Mom found the perfect place for her sweet little reptile. Years later, Dad would be sitting in the living room reading the paper and he'd come across an article about a Florida alligator chomping on a golfer or eating a poodle and he'd yell out to Mom in the kitchen, "News of Albert, Elsie! News of Albert!" and she would smile. She liked to think Albert was doing just fine, although she surely doubted her sweet baby would eat a poodle.

Just after World War II, Mom was given a baby fox by a passing hunter, and she raised it to maturity. I was just a baby then, but I remember the little creature and his narrow snout and bushy half-silver tail. He would never walk on the floor but jumped from chair to couch to the top of Dad's head, causing him to flail wildly until the fox leaped off. I couldn't stop laughing when that happened. One day, the fox disappeared mysteriously, and it broke my mom's heart. I wrote about the mystery of what happened to that little fox in *Sky of Stone*, but suffice it to say that she loved the little creature, even though it had a tendency to sample the occasional hen from the neighbor's chicken coop. Years later, Mom acquired a baby squirrel, this time from a passing lumberjack. Chipper the squirrel lived in our house for years, happily eating the family Bible and generally causing havoc by biting my brother or me whenever he got the chance. Chipper also drove our cats crazy by jumping on their backs and hurling himself onto the curtains where he'd swing, chortling, just out of paw's reach. He was a mean old squirrel we all dearly loved and provided several adventures.

There were always dogs and cats in the Hickam family and in nearly every family in town. I learned so much from them as I grew up. The dogs would follow us boys wherever we went. They'd follow us up in the mountains barking and howling as we did the same. They'd follow us down to the Big Store where they would wait patiently outside with the other town dogs while we boys had a soda pop. They were part of our boyhood gangs, playing hide-and-go-seek with us (they mostly gave our hiding places away, but we didn't much care), running along with us to the rock that marked the "straight base" in our pick-up baseball games, and playing dodgeball with us against the side of the brick company office building. We all loved our dogs, and when one of them got sick with old age or got hurt, we did everything we could to nurse them back to health. Over the years, the company doctors would occasionally be presented an old dog carried in the arms of one of us snot-nosed boys, our cheeks wet with tears. The doctors would always do what they could. I had dogs die in my arms, and I learned much about life, death and myself.

Cats were my mom's true joy. She always had a cat or two, and they slept around the house, even on the beds at night. She named the mountain behind our house after an old mother cat named Sis who liked to sun herself on a big rock up there. Lucifer, a tough, old black tomcat, came to us when I was in grade school. There was a deep wisdom in Lucifer and a gentleness that belied his name. He lived up in the mountains mostly, coming down to get the ticks picked off him and the occasional good meal. After he got really old, he took up residence in our basement near the coal-fired furnace. One time, Sherman Siers and I were up in the mountains cutting pine tree boughs for use as Christmas decorations and came upon a dying deer fawn. As recounted in *The Coalwood Way*, we kept it company until it died. When I got home and went down in the basement to get the tools to put up the boughs, I was suddenly overwhelmed by the experience. I started to cry, but all of a sudden Lucifer jumped up on the washing machine and got eye level with me. He gave me such a look that I knew he was trying to communicate. My tears vanished while I looked into those great yellow eyes and I swan that an ancient wisdom seemed to flow out of them, wisdom that said that death is as much a part of life as living.

My favorite cat was Daisy Mae, my companion during much of the Rocket Boys era. Daisy Mae would sleep on my bed, and I would often talk to her before I'd go to sleep at night. She heard all the crazy ideas I had and even a lot about the girls I kept falling in love with but who didn't love me back. Of course she couldn't reply, but she didn't have to. Just having someone listen was enough. Daisy Mae was killed by a man who was angry at my father. What that man really was, of course, was afraid because he had let his family fall apart. I wrote about him in *Rocket Boys* and how he was forced to leave town. I grieved for Daisy Mae, but ultimately I learned how much everybody in my family and Coalwood and especially the other Rocket Boys loved me by the way they supported me after she died. We all loved our animals. They lent us their strength and wisdom and helped to make us unafraid, and we did what we could for them, too.

We love our animals.
We keep our families together.
We are not afraid.

OTHER VOICES: WE KEEP OUR FAMILIES TOGETHER

She Prevailed
Roy Lee Cooke (an original Rocket Boy)

In 1955, coal was booming, and therefore Coalwood was booming, too. Like most wives in Coalwood, my mother didn't have a paying job. She took care of the household and enjoyed it. Her husband was a solid citizen of Coalwood and an active member of the Masonic lodge in Welch. Life was good. Then the world came tumbling down. While visiting Winston-Salem during the week of July Fourth, traditionally the vacation week for coal miners, her husband died suddenly at age forty-five. She sat on the side of the bed and told me my father had died. We both cried, and I asked her, "What are we going to do?" She said, "Don't worry, we're going to be fine." This woman, without a college education, who had never driven a car in her life and had never taken care of the checkbook, was now the head of the family. But she was up to the task. After the funeral was over she knew she had to take charge. She had someone drive her to the county courthouse and got the court to appoint her administrator of the estate so she had access to what little money was in the bank. She got her brother-in-law to teach her how to drive a car (and probably taught him how to cuss in the process). Then she got a job running the school lunchroom at the Coalwood School to support us. It was the rule in those days that the family of a deceased miner had to move out of company housing. Thanks to Homer Hickam (Senior), we did not have to move. Later on, she actually purchased the house from the coal company. During the five years between my father's death and my graduation from Big Creek High School, my mother provided a good home for us, showed interest in the goings-on of all the kids of the community, and she also supported the Rocket Boys. After all the things that have happened to this country on September 11 and beyond, I have contemplated the frightening things that can take place in one's lifetime. It occurs to me that having one's spouse die suddenly, leaving you without a means of support for you and your child, can be as frightening as anything there is. Carrie Gretchen Austin Cooke, my mother, had that experience. And you know, she not only endured, she prevailed.

We Just Liked Each Other
Jacky Carroll

I really don't know if the Carrolls were any greater than any other family who lived in Coalwood. Maybe we were because of our sheer numbers! Mom and Dad used to say they had six children before they knew what was causing

Mom to get pregnant. Mom said she and Dad thought it was from something in the drinking water! The other Carroll family, who also lived in the Frog Level section of Coalwood, was my dad's brother, better known to me as "Uncle Red." Red is also the father to one of the Rocket Boys, Jim O'Dell Carroll.

My brother Bobby and I and our cousins played together most every day. We grew up more like brothers than cousins. We always were together at Christmastime. My whole family would go to Uncle Red's house and watch them open their Christmas gifts, and after they had opened the last gift, we would all go to our house and they would watch us open ours. We always had self-respect, as well as respect for our friends and other families. We were honest as the day was long, very proud, hardworking, trustworthy, church-going, God-fearing people. The Carrolls walked a straight line pretty much. In addition, we had all the love a mom and dad could give a family. This is why my mom and dad were the foundation of our home. If you would replace the Carroll name and use most any other family name in Coalwood, I think the result would be about the same. The whole community was like this. We just liked each other.

An Honorable Man
Clint Senter

My grandfather, Reverend Lester Clyde Senter, was the model of a man. He was the patriarch of our family. Born and raised near Richlands, Virginia, he migrated to Cucumber, West Virginia, in the early 1900s. God gave him many gifts. Paw Paw had an extraordinary ability to do mechanical work. He could repair anything. If for some reason he didn't have the right part, he would fabricate it from scratch. He invented many timesaving devices to help him and his neighbors with difficult work. One invention Paw Paw devised was a way to cut holes in a large, circular saw so that it would bolt onto the hub of the rear axle of his truck. This way, he could jack up the truck, install the blade and, using the truck engine, run a portable sawmill.

Not all of his inventions were quite so successful. He once created a flintlock rifle (he called it his Davy Crockett squirrel gun). I was seven years old the time he tested it. He carefully moved everyone away, then loaded, tamped, set the flintlock hammer, aimed the gun and pulled the trigger. It backfired, sending a metal fragment whizzing by his right temple. He never fired the gun again.

Paw Paw, of course, was a coal miner. He worked at small mines, Bishop and what then was known as Big Auger (Jacobs Fork). He went with men to the coal seams during the day and then took men to God at night. The pride, honor, dignity, work ethic and personal character that he portrayed daily, he also unselfishly instilled in his children and his grandchildren. We stand for right, he told us, in the face of all odds.

I proudly say that whatever measure of a man I am today was directly inspired by this giant. He always put his family first, for he often said that a family is all a man really has in this world. Protecting and providing for one's family is the most honorable thing a man can do. My wish is that someday I can measure up to half his size. Better yet, when I'm gone, someone might say about me, "That boy was a lot like his Paw Paw."

Now, that's the true southern West Virginia heritage.

There Are No Perfect Parents
Willie "Billy" Rose (an original Rocket Boy)

Both of my parents, Arnie Bee and Beulah Mae "Boots" Rose, are dead now. They grew up during the Depression in our country. My father did not attend school and began working in the coal mine at the age of thirteen. My mother's parents died when she was in the fourth grade. She lived with her brothers and sisters and did not continue in school.

Even during good times when the miners worked five and six days a week, my parents and my brothers and sisters and I still had it rough. My father was an alcoholic and spent his income on things other than his family. When I went to the Coalwood School, I received plenty of help from kind and caring teachers. Mr. Likens, the principal, bought me clothes out of his pocket. I worked in the cafeteria to pay for my lunch. Many of the teachers (Mrs. Mahoney in particular) let me work in and around their homes to earn money to help myself and my family.

In 1957, I entered Big Creek High School, and my father quit his job. His pelvic area had been crushed while working in the mines. Because he no longer worked, we had to move from a nice section of Coalwood to another part of town. Our electricity was cut off, and I had to study using kerosene lamps. Teachers and administrators at Big Creek High School recognized my plight and made it easier for me by allowing me to work in the cafeteria for my lunch. During this time, I joined Sonny Hickam and the Big Creek Missile Agency and became a Rocket Boy. We got called heroes, but I don't think we were. The people who raised us and taught us, they were the heroes.

The true hero in my family was my mother. She was a hero because she would not abandon her seven children when most women would have done so. My father was an abusive husband and an abusive father. After we were old enough to understand, Mother told us that our father was not always that way. She told us he began to drink to ease the pain after his injury. Although I never asked my mother why she put up with the hell she endured, I think I know. She knew what it was like to grow up without parents, and she would not allow that to happen to us.

I have learned there are no perfect people and therefore no perfect parents. I have learned that events and people shape other people to be who and what they are. I have learned we have to be careful when we criticize the actions of others. I did not live the life my father lived. I am determined, just as my mom, to always keep my family together. It is my strength.

We Looked After Each Other
Elizabeth Burton Drees

The grade school of the little mining town of Vivian was about one half mile from the mines. Our windows faced the highway, and when there was a mine explosion, we could hear the horns blasting and see the ambulance come down the road and past the school with sirens and lights flashing. Next, there would be the dreaded knock on one of the classroom doors and the principal would call out a student's name. We knew that student would be sent home as his or her father had been killed or wounded in the explosion. All the kids lived in fear of those sounds, and I can remember my heart beating rapidly when the door opened and praying they would not call my name.

As relieved as we felt for ourselves, we also felt the pain of the children facing life without their father. The coal company would only let the family live in the company house as long as the father was an employee. The family had to find somewhere else to live. Lives were changed forever when there was an accident, but we looked after each other. All the women in the mining community would take food to the families, do their laundry, take care of the children and help them get through times of tragedy.

Surrounded by Bravery
Brenda Conn Norwood

I was surrounded by bravery while growing up in McDowell County. Two of the bravest people I ever knew were my grandmother, Amanda Frances Landy, and my mother, Louise Landy Conn. I could never put in words the invaluable lessons of survival, love, kindness and pride they taught me by just their daily living. When my mother was two years old and the youngest of four, my grandfather was killed in a mining accident. My grandmother answered a knock at the door and four miners were on her porch carrying a basket with her husband's broken remains. That bleak sorrowful night, my grandmother became a widow with four children and a fifth on the way. But I never heard my grandmother or mother complain. Grandmother raised five children by pedaling a Singer sewing machine night and day. She sewed everything from men's suits to draperies and wedding gowns. Nothing was too difficult for her.

After my grandmother passed away, my mother worked at Sears Roebuck in Welch. When I was about ten years old, we moved to a little two-bedroom house at Browns Creek with indoor plumbing. My mother stretched every dollar until it squeaked to get me the little things I needed. A traveling salesman sold us a clarinet, and she paid it off at eight dollars a month. That clarinet led me to music lessons and later joining the Welch High School Band. My heart swells with pride when I recall my childhood, all the love I felt, and never knowing I was poor in most of the world's eyes. I had a brave mother who practically pushed me out the door to seek my education as a nurse. I was blessed to have known her, my grandmother and all the wonderful people of McDowell County.

They Never Flinched
Bill Mahoney

For thirty-five years, my mother, Virginia Mahoney, was a teacher at the Coalwood School, and my dad, "Spud" Mahoney, was an outside foreman at the coal mine. They were married in 1930, a time when teachers couldn't be married. Their marriage was kept secret for a year or so until the rule was changed.

Dad had the familiar cough that most miners had, continually trying to rid his lungs of coal dust. He worked long hours and would collapse tiredly on the living room floor after supper. But when he could, he spent time with my sisters, Jane and Jill, and me. He knew how important that was. Despite her demanding schedule at school, Mother found time to take Jane and me by bus across the mountain to Welch for piano lessons. To my dislike, she even took me for Latin lessons as I grew older.

Teachers in Coalwood were leaders for the upward development of the coal miners' children. As a teacher, my mother had her work cut out for her. She often told stories of her classroom experiences. The stories would find their way into the community so other parents could appreciate them. As a teenager, I noticed young adults coming back to talk with the teachers about their appreciation for their Coalwood education. Many of life's lessons were learned there. High achievement was expected, even demanded in grammar, spelling, math, penmanship, reading and social interaction. And an absolute lesson was that if you got a spanking in school, you'd get another when you got home. No questions asked!

Christmas meant celebration in Coalwood. Trees from the mountains were brought to classrooms, plays were held, and the meaning of Christmas was woven into school activities. My sisters and I loved those times, and my parents worked to make it special. I recall one time there was a boy who was falsely known in Mother's class for making trouble, and he was even said to have stolen lunch money from a schoolmate. His life was miserable. To remedy this, the honor of going to the woods for the class Christmas tree was bestowed upon that boy by my mother. He was dumbfounded that she would lift him to this position of honor in front of his classmates. In addition, she took off her watch and placed it on his wrist so he'd know when it was time to return. Mrs. Mahoney trusted him! He was thus reinstated with his classmates and with his own self-worth. He told me later in life about this incident and its importance to him. He valued my mother as one of the two or three people most responsible for his standing tall throughout life.

My mother helped watch over the town of Coalwood. My dad helped provide the backbone for the Coalwood economy. Other parents did the same. They never flinched from what they saw as their duty. A parental network was always present, with roles established and respected. The job was not to have the children love the adults. The job was to make the children good people! Children became prepared for a world bigger than Coalwood because most folks knew, deep down, that Coalwood wouldn't last forever. Stories told by the adults to children were common and positive. It was all part of the process, a process that yielded remarkable success by producing teachers, engineers, doctors, lawyers, writers and other professionals. And it also produced good parents to continue the positive learning cycle into future generations. This was a simple time from a distant past, full of challenged people working toward life's achievements in the small mining community of Coalwood, West Virginia.

WE KEEP OUR FAMILIES TOGETHER: A SUMMARY

A good way to chase fear from your life is to build your family on the Coalwood model. Everyone needs a safe harbor, a place we can go where we know there are people who love us and depend on us, too. That harbor can be our family.

But a family is a duty, too. Once taken on, a family should be forever. Coalwood people held the family as sacred, as important as anything there was in their lives. They believed that it was necessary to keep a family intact so that all within it would know who they were and where they fit. They knew that it is especially frightening to children to not know where they belong. An intact, functioning family works to not only provide a loving refuge but also fills in the cracks of our own personalities. Where one family member is weak, another is strong. A cohesive group is always stronger than an individual, no matter how smart he is, or how many muscles he has or anything else. The family can be a shield against the world and also the springboard to a better life.

Today, there are daily assaults on the family. Movies, television and books all popularize the idea that it's all right to break up a family, just so long as nobody gets hurt. That is, of course, an impossible thing to do. Somebody always gets hurt. Actually, *everybody* gets hurt, even the person who forces the divorce. I've been divorced (no kids involved, thank goodness), and I can tell you that there is no pain quite as awful. I'm going to work hard to make sure I never have to go through another one again. Divorce is a terrible idea. The best way to avoid it is to make sure you marry the right person. Be selective and be careful. Ask yourself, would you go into business with this person? Strip away the clouds of love for just a moment and make absolutely, utterly certain that this is THE ONE.

Building a family—that's a great idea. There is something very satisfying about creating a family and keeping it going, no matter what. As the people of Coalwood instinctively knew, it is just the right thing to do. It could very well be a biological truth that we can only be happy within a family that is organized as families for eons have been—one father, one mother, a set of sequential kids. Being part of an intact family is a way to surely banish fear. If you can, get yourself inside one. You'll be the stronger for it. And once your family is built, keep it the Coalwood way.

We keep our families together.
We are not afraid.

#4

We trust in God but rely on ourselves.

The men who attacked the United States on September 11, 2001, believed they could kill people because they had special insight into the mind of God. Their God was a supernatural being so mean and angry that it demanded blood because it and its holy places weren't getting the proper respect. It was also a God so weak that it had to make promises to the murderers that they'd get a good deal in paradise if they butchered innocents in its name. Such a concept of the Creator of our universe is as idiotic as it is sad. To believe such things doesn't make any sense, but it does indicate minds that have stopped working, except for being afraid of the real world. Sometimes, being afraid can make a man or a woman turn to a religion that promises eternal happiness if only they pledge to leave their families, or give away their lives and money, or do awful and destructive things. But that isn't a religion. That's evil and stupidity disguised as a religion. It is beyond me how anyone could think that the same God who made this glorious universe and this magnificent world could be so small-minded as to indulge in murder. What in heaven's name were these men on September 11 thinking—or, more to the point, *not* thinking? All I can conclude is that they were so terrified of life that they threw theirs away and for nothing. They had become men as twisted and frightened as the beliefs they held. Religion is a good thing, but like all things, it can be carried too far. It is proper to adore the Creator of us all. But that Creator also gave us brains to think and reason, and we ought to use them, even when they seem to disagree with the religious doctrines we otherwise hold as holy.

The people of Coalwood figured every man had a right to his own religion and beliefs, but they appreciated it if he went about it with as little fuss as possible. Over the years, the churches in Coalwood changed their religions to suit the needs of the coal company. Sometimes the preachers brought in were Pentecostals, and sometimes Baptists, and other times Methodists. The Catholics went over the mountain to the church in Welch. Jews went all the way to Bluefield. When it came to religion, Coalwood had figured out a long time ago there was more than one way to get to heaven. Preachers and priests and rabbis weighed in with their thoughts from the pulpit, and they were always given a respectful hearing, but in the quiet of the night, when all they could hear were the beating of their own hearts in tune with their souls, southern West Virginians tended to make their own judgments about the nature of God. Their beliefs were based on not only what they heard or read, but also on what they sensed every day by the evidence of creation all around them, from the vast, unending, glorious mountains to the deep, dangerous coal mine that always sat waiting. They believed and trusted in God, but they had also concluded that He was under no obligation to give them anything. For that, a willingness to work hard and sweat a little was required.

If there was a favorite part of the Bible for most of Coalwood's folks, it was a verse out of Matthew that said "Not everyone who says to me 'Lord, Lord' shall enter the kingdom of heaven, but he who does the will of my Father in heaven." What that meant to them was that a man who prayed out loud and made a big show of his religion didn't amount to much. The better man was the one who quietly did good works, while not forgetting it was the good Lord who gave him the ability to do it. It was the religion of the confident and brave, not the puffed up or sly who figured to get a reward for his piety, either on Earth or in heaven.

The people of Coalwood were against calling on God any time they needed help. For one thing, it was considered impolite. God had a lot of things to worry about, after all, without including everything that got in the way of any one particular human being. The way folks in the town saw it, God had already provided them with most of what they needed to get past a scrape, including their own good common sense. They reserved their prayers mostly for thanking the good Lord, to let Him know they appreciated the abundance He'd given them, and also blessing others. They would have laughed at a preacher who promised to get them eternal salvation if only they gave him their money. And had there ever been a preacher so foolish as to promise them gifts in heaven if only they killed unbelievers, he might have gotten himself smacked around and carried over to Welch and thrown in the county jail. He'd have probably ended up in a mental institution, too. The attitude of Coalwood was to admire the Almighty and all His works, but ultimately to rely on their own native intelligence and hard work to get through and enjoy life. Religion didn't lead Coalwood people off to do bad and stupid things in God's name, either. The God they worshiped was as good and strong and unafraid as they were.

> *We trust in God but rely on ourselves.*
> *We are not afraid.*

WE KNOW YOU DON'T LEARN EVERYTHING ABOUT GOD IN CHURCH

My father wasn't much for going to church. He liked to say his religion was his own business, and he didn't need to listen to a preacher try to convince him of another view. At the same time, Dad thought it was really important that my brother Jim and I go to church. "You've got to learn what it says in the Bible, little men," he'd say. "It's a great book, and our civilization stands on it." He actually said it that way. I didn't know what he meant, but it sounded grand enough to convince me to go happily to church, whether Dad went or not.

One time, when I was six years old, I did a really stupid thing. I was always intrigued by the old mine shaft down from the tipple. It was inside a locked shed, but every so often I'd find the shed unlocked and go inside. The shaft was big and round and steam rose up out of it. It was fun to throw a rock down it and listen, many seconds later, when it hit the abandoned tunnel nearly seven hundred feet below. One day I was out playing with my dog, Littlebit. Littlebit was a tiny, black dog with a perpetual grin on his face. I loved that little dog, and he followed me everywhere I went. When I went up by the mine, I noticed that the shed over the old shaft was unlocked. I sneaked inside and threw rocks down the deep hole while Littlebit watched. After awhile, throwing rocks got to be boring so I went home, Littlebit trotting beside me. A few hours later, I realized I hadn't seen Littlebit for awhile. That night, to my astonishment and anguish, Dad brought Littlebit's limp body home. He had been found at the bottom of the old shaft by an inspector. Dad put the question to me: Had I been in the old shack? I confessed I had, but I couldn't imagine why Littlebit had returned. "Because you taught him that it was okay to go in there," Dad said. I knew he was right.

Mom ordered Dad to turn me over his knee. He did, and he gave me three good whacks. It was the only time he ever spanked me. Then he helped me bury Littlebit on the other side of the railroad tracks, just down from our house.

After I was done tamping the soil on Littlebit's grave, Dad said I should say a prayer. I had been crying steadily but now I got impudent, don't ask me why. "Dear God," I said. "Please kill me because it was my fault Littlebit got killed."

"That's a terrible prayer!" Dad gasped. "Do it over. Pray for Littlebit's soul or something."

"All right," I said, dutifully. "Dear God, please let Littlebit's soul be happy in heaven, and please don't kill me even though I deserve it."

Dad was visibly shaken. His jaw was ajar, his crisp blue eyes wide. "Gawdalmighty, Sonny, what do they teach you in that church?" He plopped his helmet back on. "Come on. Let's go see what your mom's got for supper."

Later that night, I got a rare visit from my father. Jim was asleep in the bunk bed below, but Dad found me awake. He asked me how I was doing, and I told him I had taken back my second prayer, the one that had let me off the hook, and was just waiting for my first prayer to come into play. "I'm ready to go to heaven." I knew very well what I was doing. It hurt Dad to hear me say what I did. I was getting back at him for the three whacks. Dad would have said it was the Lavender in me. Mom would have said it was the Hickam. I think it was the combination.

"Well, you can't go to heaven and that's all there is to it," Dad replied, reasonably. "You've got to stay down here with me and your mother and Jim, too, whether you like it or not."

I stuck to my guns. "I deserve a terrible thing to happen to me."

Dad looked a little nervous. "Look, Sonny, you got to stop talking this way."

"God should kill me," I said, stubbornly. I was really into it.

Mom came in just then. Maybe she'd been there the whole time. "You got to get Sonny's prayer undone, Homer."

"Well, how can I do that, Elsie?"

"You have to make a more powerful prayer, that's how."

Dad opened his mouth, then closed it. He took a deep breath, then let it out. He put his hand to his face, then let it drop. I had never seen my dad look so stricken. It filled me with vast satisfaction.

"Come on, Homer," Mom said. "God's waiting. Sonny is, too."

Finally, Dad bowed his head. "God, Sonny is a good boy, even if sometimes he acts kind of stu . . ." He stopped and started over again. "God, sometimes a boy will say something he doesn't mean. Now, you know me. I'm this boy's father. I don't go to church every Sunday . . ."

"There's truth," Mom said, crossing her arms.

Dad frowned at her, then went on. "I don't go to church every Sunday, but I'm glad to send my boys. They learn a few things there, and when they grow up, they can make up their own minds on religion. Like I have, don't you see?"

"Homer," Mom said, sighing, "this prayer's not about you."

"Give me time, woman," Dad snapped. He kept going. "Now, you know how I feel. I've got a lot to thank you for and I hope I do it often enough, in my own way. But, look now, if something ever happened to one of my boys . . . Sonny here misses his dog, and he's asked for an awful price for making a mistake, but I know you won't let that happen. If he ever got killed or anything, his mother and I would miss him our whole lives and our hearts would just about break, I guess. So let his prayer be undone."

What I said next just jumped right out of me. I surprised myself saying it, it came out so fast. It was like somebody squeezed my stomach to make it pop out. "I take it all back," I said with a little gasp. "I don't want to die. I sure am sorry about Littlebit, but I want to stay here with Mom and Dad. And even Jim, too."

Relief spread across Dad's features. Mom came up beside him and took his arm. "Pretty good, Homer," she said. "I didn't know you had it in you."

Dad puffed up, just the tiniest amount. "Well, Elsie, you don't learn everything about God in church," he replied.

Of course, since Dad didn't go to church, that meant my mom had to take us, something she was proud to do since she was going anyway. Every so often, she'd get her back up, though, and make Dad go along. He celebrated being in God's house mostly by dozing through the sermon. I looked over one time and saw he was asleep with one eye open, that eye on my mom. He wanted to make sure she knew he was unimpressed by the sermon, I guess. It was hard to figure out what the two of them were up to, most of the time. I still enjoyed watching them at it, whatever it was.

When I was seven years old, my dad was diagnosed with an awful cancer. Although my mom tried to hide it from me and Jim, it came out sooner or later as all secrets in Coalwood did, given time. I had one of my many clues when a lady spied me and Mom in the Big Store and came over and actually started to cry at the sight of me. I think she would have even hugged me had I not beat a hasty retreat behind my mother. "Poor child," she said. "He'll miss his daddy."

"His daddy is just over in the hospital," Mom replied fiercely. "And he'll be home soon."

The lady looked doubtful and went on her way. Then a man came up to Mom. "I gave blood to Homer yesterday," he said. "Then I went in to see him. He said he didn't know what he was supposed to do with all that Democrat blood." The man chuckled. "I told him, the next thing you know, Homer, you'll be voting for Harry Truman."

My mom produced a tight smile but said she doubted that was a possibility. After everybody in the Big Store got their say in, I asked Mom what was wrong with my daddy. Mom fumed a bit, then said, "He's got cancer of the colon." Then she steered me over to the butcher shop. "Got any intestines?" she asked. When the butcher said of course he did, she said, "Haul them out. Sonny needs to see what they look like." The butcher did, and Mom pointed and said, "We've all got stuff like this in us. Intestines are used to digest our food. Your daddy's intestines, the big ones lower down called the colon, have a growth in them. It's made him pretty sick."

I looked at the intestines in the butcher's hands and listened to my mom's explanation and then said, "Does anybody really eat those things?"

The butcher laughed. "You'd be surprised, Sonny," he said.

At church, it seemed every sermon included a prayer for Dad. All the Sunday school classes started with a prayer for him, too. As far as I could tell, the whole town started and ended everything it did with a prayer for my father. When we went to visit him at the hospital, Mom told him about the prayers. "I guess they can't hurt," Dad said, looking awfully weak.

"Well, Homer, I think they'll do more than that," she said.

Dad shrugged against his propped-up pillow. "The way I see it, Elsie, a man's will to live is what gets him through tough times."

"People are going out of their way to say a prayer for you," Mom told him. "You be grateful!"

Dad promised he would be as grateful as he could manage but he wasn't so sick he still couldn't have his own opinion.

On the drive back home, Mom told Jim and me we had to be strong, and she started crying. I worried she was going to run us off the road. She wasn't a great driver anyway, and what with crying, she didn't get any better. After awhile, she said, "Your dad's going to have an operation in a few days. It'll either work or it won't."

I figured out pretty quick that meant Dad would either live or die. Jim figured it out, too. He just sat there, a serious expression on his face. I had to do something different so I started whimpering. Mom said, "Now, stop it. I told you we have to be strong."

My whimpering stopped abruptly. Coalwood boy that I was, I tended to do what I was told by my parents, at least while I was in sight of one of them. "Isn't there something we can do?" I asked.

"Pray," she said. "Pray like you've never prayed before."

"Dad said prayer didn't matter as much as the will to live," I responded smartly.

"Your dad . . ." Mom took a deep breath. "Your dad has got his ways but that doesn't mean he's always right. Being right is my job. Now pray!"

After we got home, I put my mind to Mom's directive. Since she had said to pray like I'd never done it before, I decided not to just ask God to help Dad out. I would talk to God, just like I'd talk to one of my friends like Roy Lee or Benny. I talked to him about my teacher at school, Mrs. Brown, and how much I liked her. I talked to Him about Dandy, our dog, and said he was funny when he chased rabbits because he never caught one. I talked to him about Billy Hardin and how he was the smartest boy in Coalwood because he was building his own radio. Every once in awhile in all my talking, I'd also sneak in a comment that maybe God might want to help my dad get through his operation. I said that Dad was a good man at work, and the Captain needed him because God surely knew how important the Captain was. I also told God that Mom loved Dad a lot, and Jim and I did, too, and how much it would hurt not to have him around. I really put my mind to my talks with God. Sometimes, I'd try them out on Sis, our mama cat, before I let God get the latest word from Sonny Hickam. I even advised God on his business, suggesting that it would be a good example for other people to have Dad get through his operation, considering all the prayers that were being said. I mean, how would it look if Dad didn't make it after all those prayers? People might say praying wasn't worth the time and forget all about talking to God. "So, see, God," I'd say, "it's best for everybody and you, too, that Dad get well." I thought God enjoyed our conversations, don't ask me why, so I determined to keep them up.

The trouble was that after awhile I ran out of things to report to God. After all, there was only just so much that was happening around a seven-year-old in Coalwood, West Virginia. Accordingly, I went to my buddy, Roy Lee. Roy Lee always knew what to do, no matter what the problem was. He listened and suggested that maybe I ought to start telling jokes to God. "God needs a laugh now and again," he said authoritatively.

It made sense to me, so Roy Lee began to tell me jokes he thought were appropriate for God, and I passed them on. I have to say, of all my talks with God, I think the joke ones were the ones He liked the best. I could just sense it, some-how, with a warm feeling that came over me.

The night before Dad's operation, Mom and Jim and I went to see him. For some reason, Dad and I were left alone in his room for a few minutes, and I volunteered the infor-mation about my talks with God. But then I worried that maybe Dad should have attended church more than he did. Dad answered, "Living is a thing mostly earned, Sonny. I have the best doctors in the world. I got all the Democrat blood in the county ready to mix with my Republican when

I need it. I got a good reason to stick around, seeing as how Jim isn't old enough and you aren't smart enough yet to take care of your mother. So don't you worry about me and God. We're fine, Him and me."

I had to agree I wasn't smart enough to take care of my mother, and I seriously doubted anyone in the world was that smart, except maybe my dad. Then I told him I was telling jokes to God on his behalf. "Roy Lee's telling them to me first but they're all religious," I assured Dad since he knew what kind of boy Roy Lee could be.

Dad perked up, looked at me for a long second, and then asked me to tell him one of the jokes Roy Lee and I thought were worthy of God. "Well," I said, "here's one. There was this preacher, and it was his job to sprinkle water on babies and give them their names."

"He christened them," Dad said.

"Christened them, yes sir." I kept going. Jokes only worked, Roy Lee said, if you didn't let yourself get interrupted. "Now, this was a preacher who liked to tell the future of the babies he sprinkled. One day, a mother and father came up to the front of the church, carrying their baby. The preacher took one look at the baby and said that this was the greatest baby he'd ever seen, that it was going to grow up and be a general in the United States Army, and that it would kill every mean and low thing in the world, and that we could all rest easy, seeing as how this baby was going to be the greatest soldier on Earth. When the preacher finally talked himself out, he asked, 'What's his name?' and prepared to sprinkle on the water. The father cleared his throat, leaned over and said, 'Sarah Jane.'"

Dad blinked a couple of times, and then he started to

shake. I thought he was going to fall out of his bed. Then he laughed a great laugh, threw back his head in a howl. A nurse came running in, but Dad waved her away. "Sonny just told me a joke he thought was good enough for God," he said. "And I think it's mighty close."

The nurse shooed me outside, but I could still hear Dad chuckling. I told Mom my joke, and she got a puzzled look on her face. "What's wrong with that name?" she wondered. "Sarah Jane's a perfectly good name."

I told her I agreed and left it at that. A joke that has to be explained isn't much of a joke. I was only seven years old but I knew that much already.

Dad had his operation, and three weeks later he was back to work, pulling shifts and going full blast like nothing had ever happened. It was an amazing recovery. Most everybody in Coalwood put it down to prayer. Dad put it down to his doctors, and though he hated to admit it, he said maybe all that Democrat blood helped a little, too. Mom said Dad was too stubborn to die. As for me, I was just glad I'd sent Roy Lee's jokes up to heaven. After all, even God can use a laugh, now and again.

We know you don't learn everything about God in church.
We trust in God but rely on ourselves.
We are not afraid.

WE TEACH
OUR CHILDREN WHAT'S TRUE

By the mid-1950s, the people of Coalwood had managed to build themselves as nice a little town as ever existed in the coalfields of southern West Virginia. They had a coal mine humming along that kept everybody gainfully employed. Across the mountain, Caretta was much the same. The people in both towns were pretty much satisfied. There was even union peace, while all around the county, in other coal towns, there were strikes and bloody heads. Coalwood was an oasis of peace, and prosperity. But it was during this time, when things were at their best, that it dawned on most adults in Coalwood that their children would have to leave the town as soon as they finished high school. The country's steel mills were starting to feel a lot of pressure from overseas steel production, and all of Coalwood's coal went to American steel mills. It was, people said amongst themselves, only a matter of time before steel went down and Coalwood went with it. Almost as a mantra, most of Coalwood's children began to hear at home that they needed to figure on going to college. This came, for the most part, from a people who had never even been on a college campus.

Every family handled the education of their children in a different way. It was my mother who drummed the idea of college into my brother's head, and then mine, too. There was a lot of doubt about whether I had the brains for college, but my mom kept prompting me to give it some thought, to try to figure out *something* I might be able to study to make a living. She also saw to it that I received piano lessons from

Mrs. Dantzler. Mrs. Dantzler always said I had a lot of skill. I noticed after a few dozen times of her saying that to my mom that she kept leaving off saying I had any talent. I didn't have any, so maybe that's why she left it off. Still, I learned to play the piano as well as I could, and that made me inordinately proud. Twice a year, Mrs. Dantzler held a recital at the Coalwood School, and all the parents of her students, and not a few interested bystanders, showed up to see us go through our program. I learned to sit up straight during my playing and to stand and bow properly at the end. It was all a confidence-builder, which was a good thing as I'm sure my playing left several long-dead composers frowning in their graves. But it was a bit of evidence that the coal mine wasn't in my future. What did a coal miner need with learning to play the piano and bowing and such? Not much, I suspected. I was headed out of Coalwood and with me was going nearly every other child.

Much of my book *Rocket Boys* (also known as *October Sky*) tells how it transpired that my mother finally got through to me that I would have to leave Coalwood, and how my learning to build rockets caused all kinds of commotion within my family and the whole town, too. That was during the years 1957 to 1960 when my father was about the only man left in town who thought the mine and Coalwood had a future. Dad hoped that I would become a mining engineer and come back to Coalwood to take his place as the superintendent, but since I had my mind made up about working in space, a conflict rose between us. Eventually, I left Coalwood and went to college, as did nearly every other child in my class at school. We did it in a variety of ways. Some got scholarships (I didn't—that was just movie magic in the film *October Sky*), some went into the military so they could use the GI Bill, and others simply worked their way through. But we went, and that was the main thing.

To go to college and do well meant that students from Coalwood and all over southern West Virginia needed to learn the truth in our education, the scientific truth of the nature of the Earth and the universe. If we didn't know those things, we'd never get through our college studies. Religious study had its place, but that place wasn't in the schools. Since nearly all the students were churchgoers, sometimes religion and academic studies naturally bumped up against each other. It just couldn't be helped.

I had survived algebra in the tenth grade, barely managing a B after a flurry of good test scores at the end of the school year. But in the eleventh grade, I got good scores in geometry from the start. I thought there was something marvelous about geometry, more than what it said in the textbook. I loved to just let my mind go and soar the endless reaches of space where lines crossed to create points with no dimensions at all and parallel lines intersected in infinity. Studying geometry got me to thinking a lot about infinity, and what it was like there, and how all the postulates and theorems and principles of geometry were true across all the universe. I lay in bed at night, my cat Daisy Mae at my feet, and looked up into the darkness and allowed my mind to go wherever it wanted to go. Sometimes when I did that I actually felt like I was flying, soaring into the night sky over Coalwood and through the dark valleys and mountain hollows that marched away into the moonlight. One night, when I was having one of these visions, I had the startling revelation that geometry was, in fact, a message from God.

My mind closed down, and I came immediately back to my bed, my room coalescing around me, my desk and chair, my little chest of drawers, the books and model airplanes suddenly so terribly real. Daisy Mae stirred and I knew I was safe in my room, where I felt the safest of anywhere, but I was still trembling with fear. I lay there, unsleeping, waiting for the idea to leave me, but it wouldn't. All the next day and the next, it kept batting around in my head. I decided I had better go and see a preacher about it.

Reverend Lanier of the Coalwood Community Church greeted me warily in his study. He had preached a sermon to the company about letting us boys have a slack dump to launch our rockets. His sermon had been successful and he still had his job, but it had been a close call seeing as how he'd taken a deviation from the company line. Nevertheless, Reverend Lanier heard me out as I presented my revelation that in the principles and theorems and axioms of geometry, God had sent us a message of truth. Reverend Lanier wasn't buying it. "You're talking about arithmetic, Sonny," he said and tapped the Bible. "All of God's truth is here, in the Good Book."

I tried to talk about it some more with him, but Reverend Lanier just kept tapping the Bible. My next stop was the Reverend Richard at the Mudhole Church of Distinct Christianity. He and I walked down the narrow aisle of his tiny church toward the altar while I explained my idea that all the theorems, axioms and principles in my geometry book were ones that God had thought up. The Reverend seemed to bow under the weight of what I was saying. "Gawdalmighty," he breathed. "Can't be nothing but God's plan." He grabbed a Bible from behind his pulpit and plumped down on one of the crude wooden pews. I sat beside him while he opened the book and closed it and then opened it again. "The Word is the Word, Sonny," he said, running his finger along a random passage. "But the Number is God's, too. Got to be." He scratched his chin, his eyes lifted to the plain wooden cross nailed to the wall by the choir box. Then he looked at me. "How did you come to think about this?"

I shrugged. "It was in the dark, just before I went to sleep. All of a sudden, there it was."

The Reverend nodded his head, as if it all made sense to him now. "Yes, we're always closest to God just before we doze off," he said, and he began to ponder. After a bit, he said, "Sonny, the day may come when people honor you and say how smart you are. But don't you pay any mind to it." He leaned his head toward the cross. "All the glory in the world belongs right there."

I looked at the cross and then bowed my head, suddenly afraid that God might punish me for poking around in His business. "Yes, sir," I gulped.

"Don't be putting on any airs, getting prideful and all," the Reverend admonished.

"No, sir," I said in a voice as small as I felt.

Then Reverend Richard laughed. "Boy, don't you be fretting. God is love, don't you know that? He ain't never going to hurt you. He's got plans for you. That's why He told you about his geometry."

I nodded dumbly. "Then go on with you," he said. "I got some praying to do. A boy in Coalwood finding the Word of God in his geometry book. Yes, sir. I got a lot of praying to do about *that*."

I went back to studying geometry, but I never forgot that the Reverend Richard had agreed with me that God was a mathematician, too, the greatest one of all. It made my studies all the easier.

Two years later, when I was a senior in high school, one of our teachers made another demonstration of how God and scientific truth are all right together. There was a sophomore girl, one Inell Crawford, who'd taken exception to a mention of Darwin's theories of evolution in her biology book. Her preacher wouldn't hold with it, she told Coach Mams, who was at the time not only the head football coach but also the school biology teacher. Coach Mams replied that what Inell said was just fine, that she could just ignore that part in the book about evolution, but she'd best keep studying frog intestines or she was going to fail his class. That settled things to everybody's satisfaction until a boy in her class, a boy who had pretensions of some day being a great scientist, accosted Inell in the hall, giving her grief about her "stupid" religion. His name was Preston Yates, and Charles Darwin was one of his gods. The next thing anybody knew they were yelling at each other. That lasted about five seconds, until Mr. Turner, the principal, showed up. Inell and Preston were sent flying to their next class.

When Coach Mams heard about the fracas, he called Inell and Preston into his classroom. "Debate is healthy," he told them. "But yelling in the hall is not. Here's the way we're going to do this. We're going to have a formal debate. But Mr. Yates, you'll take the side of the Bible, and Miss Crawford, you will take the side of Darwin. Let's see how sharp your intellectual powers are. Can you take the opposing side and win?"

Preston and Inell accepted the challenge, and two weeks
later the debate was held after school in Coach Mams's classroom. Everybody interested crowded in to hear the debate.
That included me. Preston sat in his corner as did Inell in
hers. Inell was up first. She gave a condensation of Mr.
Darwin's book, said how complex it was, and how he had
such fine powers of logic. She said it *was* all logical, that it
sure did look like animals had changed over time. Then she
went on, citing the geological records as proof that the Earth
had been around for millions of years and so had animals and
plants. The fossil record showed that animals and plants
were a lot different now than they used to be. She held up
fossils of ferns her daddy had found in the coal mine, ferns
that didn't live anywhere near West Virginia anymore. She
showed pictures of animal fossils and said those animals had
gone extinct long ago. She said there were a lot of animals
alive today that hadn't existed way back when. The only logical conclusion, she said, was that animals changed because
of their environment and turned into new animals to get by.
She was near tears when she finished, her voice trembling. I
felt sorry for her. I thought maybe she had lost her faith in
God by the hard work she'd done for her side of the debate.

When Inell sat down, Preston stood up, holding the Holy
Bible. He looked pretty upset, too. He said that he'd looked
into the Bible, studied it up and down, and he thought there
was so much truth in it, that he didn't see how it could also
have any lies. Unless all the Bible was absolutely to the letter the truth, Preston said, then all of it was a lie, and he just
couldn't imagine that the millions of people who believed
in the Bible and built great churches and cathedrals could
be that wrong. Darwin must have lied, Preston said, even

though he didn't mean to do it. Preston was sweating by then and looking very sad. I was afraid he'd convinced himself that science was wrong, and he couldn't be a scientist.

Coach Mams questioned each debater carefully to see the extent of their knowledge. He had *Origin of the Species* on one side of his desk and the Holy Bible on the other. He referred to each and was satisfied that both students had delved deeply into the opposing texts. Then he looked at Preston sternly and said, "Mr. Yates, do you really think Darwin is wrong?" And he looked at Inell just as sternly and said, "And do you really think he is right?" When neither student replied, Coach Mams said, "The truth is the truth, it can't be changed to be anything else. But the truth is not always what it seems." He put one hand on *Origin*. "This book is the truth as it appears to be." He put his other hand on the Bible. "But this book is the truth that is *more* than what things seem to be. Do you understand?"

Inell and Preston both shook their heads. They didn't understand, not at all. Neither did I. Coach Mams continued. "Preston, a scientist must know the truth as it appears to be. This is not only true for evolution and biology. It is true for all the sciences. The scientist experiments and writes down the results of what he can measure. To do anything else is to tell a lie. But he has a brain that is designed to look past what he knows, to speculate as to what the larger truth is from all that he has measured. That's what Mr. Darwin did. He speculated, and he concluded." Coach Mams tapped the side of his head. "He used the brains God gave him."

Coach Mams patted the Bible. "Inell, this is more than a book. This is wisdom, the knowledge of life beyond what can be measured. When you read things in this book, you are reading past what can be seen with our senses and all the measuring devices we might invent."

Coach Mams picked up both books, put *Origin* under the Bible and placed them gently in the center of his desk. "These books together," he said, "tell the truth of that which can be measured and that which can't. Even though I am both a scientist and a religious man, I see no conflict between them. They are both works of the Lord."

Quentin Wilson, the brains of the Big Creek Missile Agency, was sitting beside me. He raised his hand. "So who won the debate, Coach?" he demanded.

"Everybody who just understood what I said, Mr. Wilson," Coach Mams said with a smile.

I thought I understood. It looked like Preston and Inell did, too. They were giving each other sympathetic glances. At least, I thought they were sympathetic. The next time I saw them they were in the gymnasium at lunch, holding hands. They went to the Christmas Formal together, too.

> *We teach our children what's true.*
> *We trust in God but rely on ourselves.*
> *We are not afraid.*

WE UNDERSTAND GOD MADE US TO GRIEVE DEEP, SHARP AND SHORT

Faith in a Creator means a belief that there is a Great Someone who built the universe and we're part of His family. It's a good feeling to have such faith. Just as living in an intact family makes us feel good, we feel most comfortable in an intact universe, too. To banish fear, some say the thing to do is just believe that there is an almighty deity loose in the cosmos and all will be well. I think there's a lot of truth to that. But be careful when they tell you that you'd best not question things because if you do you're going off to hell. I've never believed that was right. Since we can, shouldn't we ponder the nature and purpose of our Creator and not just believe what somebody else has to say about Him? I think so, but it's my opinion. Don't believe me. Use your own brain to come to your personal conclusion. If you do, it'll help you to be strong and unafraid.

The people of Coalwood figured they were mostly about the Lord's business, at least in their own way and in their own time. They worked hard to be able to handle any situation, good or bad, but they trusted the Lord would help them figure out the things they needed to do. At the mine, the men were well trained to handle any emergency and were confident that their supervisors would arrange things to be as safe as possible. Still, a lot of miners said a prayer when they went down the shaft and got on the man-trip to go into work. They relied on themselves and their bosses, but they didn't think it hurt to check in with the Lord from time to time, just to give thanks and to advise Him they were still on the job and hoped He was, too.

In 1955, when I was twelve years old, there was an accident in the mine. The accident, an explosion of a pillar of coal that miners called a "bump," instantly killed a young man who was well liked and respected. But after the funeral, life quickly got back to normal in Coalwood. Men went to work, women cleaned the houses and shopped at the company stores, and kids went to school. The grieving that was done when someone was killed in the mine was done the Coalwood way—quickly with a minimum of fuss, and as privately as possible.

For some reason, this time I found myself deeply affected and couldn't accept the usual way of grieving. I had known the young man fairly well. He was from a well-established Coalwood family. He was unmarried and lived in the Club House with the rest of the bachelor miners in town. He had played first-string football at the high school. Lots of pretty Coalwood girls figured to tie him down, one year or the next. He was one of my scoutmasters and had tried in vain to teach me to tie a bowline knot and a half-hitch. In fact, he'd tried to help me learn my knots just the night before he died. Maybe that was why I took his death personally, because I'd just been taught something by him. The way I took his passing surprised me as much as anybody, but I just couldn't help it. He was a good man and hadn't deserved to die, and I thought everybody should moan and cry about it. That's what I felt like doing, and so I did it.

Every night I went to sleep choking back my tears, and every morning I woke up doing the same. Pretty soon, I was weighed down by anguish. I put on a long face and kept my lip stuck out. I was not a pretty sight. I just kept feeling awful. I couldn't understand why everybody else in

Coalwood didn't feel as awful as me. Although my father was too busy to take any note of my whimpering, my mother observed it and was not much impressed. She decided I needed help, and so she went to the town doctor.

Doc Lassiter was one of the most respected and admired men in Coalwood. When next he spied me, just as I was coming out of the post office with our mail, he grabbed me hard by the shoulder and demanded to know what my problem was. When I told him, he snapped, "And what do you think you can change by all your moaning and groaning? Name me one thing, young man. Just one."

I thought about it and couldn't name a thing. I tried, but I just couldn't come up with anything other than it made me feel better, which I suspected was not the answer the doctor was after.

He followed up his question with an admonition: "Listen to me very carefully. If you spread grief out and let it get a hold of your soul, it will make you as dead as the person who's been lost. Now, you get yourself up in the mountains and sob your heart out, cry a creek of tears, and bang your head against a tree. Do whatever you need to do, but go where you can't be seen—I won't have you scaring the ladies and the other children—and get it out double quick lest you can't ever get it out. Grieve deep, sharp and short, that's our style! Why? Because to do it any other way is to tear yourself up inside so much, you'll never recover."

Although I didn't instantly accept the doctor's words, I knew that I had made enough of a spectacle of myself and put away my overt grief. Now, nearly fifty years later, after witnessing death firsthand in war and having my father die, and losing so many others I have loved, I have come to

believe the good doctor was correct and the Coalwood way
to grieve is the right way. It seems to me, in this country we
have nearly made grief into a spectacle akin to entertainment. We have learned by examples we have seen on television and movies that we should mourn openly, loudly and for
a very long time with anguished demands for "closure," as if
there were such a thing as bringing death and loss into some
sort of full circle where everything is all right again. The
people of Coalwood who raised me saw such displays as not
only undignified but dangerous, too. If we think we can go
on with our grief until something miraculous happens that
makes it all right, grief will have time to take up residence in
our hearts. Grief can become a habit, just like fear and
dread. In fact, long-term grief is just another way of being
afraid. It is far better to pour out our tears and anguish
quickly and then take control and get our lives going again
with quiet dignity.

Recall Doc Lassiter's question to me: "What do you think
you can change with all your moaning and groaning around?"

"Nothing" was the answer I had to give then. "Nothing" is
the answer now. "Nothing" will forever be the answer. It's a
tough answer, but it is a true answer. This doesn't mean we
can't keep the people who have died in our hearts, but it
does mean that it does them or us no good to keep on being
sad about it. That's just the truth. And if there was ever anything the people of Coalwood relied on, it was the truth, no
matter how hard it seemed. It was their strength, their armor
against fear.

*We understand God made us to grieve deep, sharp and
      short.*
We trust in God but rely on ourselves.
We are not afraid.

WE WORK HARD, DO RIGHT AND LET THE LORD TAKE CARE OF THE REST

When I came home from college after my freshman year, I ended up working in Coalwood's mine in the toughest, dirtiest job my father could think up for me to do. All that summer's events, many and mysterious, are told in my book *Sky of Stone,* but I did leave a story or two out that told something of Coalwood's perspective on the nature of God.

I worked that summer with two men, one a college student like myself, the other a miner with decades of experience. My fellow student was Bobby Likens, who was also the son of the Coalwood School principal. Bobby was doing the same thing I was, working to get some money for college. He'd already graduated from Emory and Henry College and was headed to West Virginia University in the fall to go to medical school. I was at Virginia Tech, still determined to get through its engineering curriculum. Johnny Basso was an Italian immigrant who'd come to Coalwood and stayed, a bulwark of the community. Bobby and I had been apprenticed to Johnny for the summer. His job was to work us as hard as he could. As soon as we got off the man-trip in the morning, Johnny would kneel and say a silent prayer, urging Bobby and me to do the same. Bobby and I, as college boys, were of course too sophisticated to be seen kneeling and praying, even in a coal mine where nobody could see us. When we told him we weren't going to pray, Johnny regarded us for a long second. "Boys, there's only two things that are going to keep you alive in this mine," he said. "Me and the tolerance of God!"

Bobby and I still didn't pray. Worse, Bobby couldn't leave it alone. "What do you pray for, Johnny? To stay safe down here?"

Johnny said, "Why, no, Bobby. I pray that we work hard and do right for the company all day. The Lord will take care of the rest."

Bobby and I looked at each other, our lights flashing in our eyes, and tried not to smirk too much.

It didn't take too long before I nearly got myself killed in the mine. We were removing old posts, timbers that held up the roof of the mine, when I took out one that had been holding up a kettle bottom. Kettle bottoms are the fossils of old tree stumps and tend to fall without warning. Johnny saw where I was and, at the last instant, knocked me aside just as the kettle bottom dropped. It came down with a thunderous roar, hitting the ground like a sledge hammer. I picked myself up, then looked over and saw Johnny had gotten no farther than his knees. "Praise God," he said, aloud, "and all His wonders." Bobby just stood there, stunned by what had happened.

"You saved my life, Johnny!" I blurted.

Johnny opened one eye. "God saved you. Now give up thanks to Him for it."

I just stood there. I couldn't do it. It was too embarrassing.

All summer, Bobby and I worked with Johnny. After awhile, we were assigned the particularly arduous job of laying down railroad track. It was as rough a job as existed in the mine. Every day, we assaulted the track like the lives of men depended on it, which they did. If that track wasn't laid perfectly, a car could come off a rail and maybe turn over. Men could die when that happened. Johnny kept Bobby and me working hard and fast, but with care. Every tie, every rail, every spike had to go in perfectly. Johnny prayed every day before we started and every day when we stopped, too. Bobby and I just watched him do it.

One day, our foreman came to us and said Johnny wouldn't be with us that day, or the next one either. My dad had sent him over to the Caretta mine to work with one of the new foremen who was having trouble with his section. It seemed Johnny was a wonderful teacher of more than college boys.

Bobby and I went to the section where we were laying track. As we picked up our tools, Bobby surprised me when he said, "Maybe we ought to say a little prayer."

It was an opportunity to show Bobby what a true sophisticate I was. I laughed out loud. "Come on, let's go to work."

And we did. It proved to be the worst day we ever had in the mine. Nothing went right. Spikes bent when we hit them, and rails rolled over on our toes. I tripped over a barrel of spikes and fell on my face. I got a big splinter in my hand from a tie. Bobby got to practice being a doctor by drawing it out. I didn't much like his technique and told him so. "I haven't been to medical school yet," he pointed out unnecessarily.

At the end of the day we'd laid mighty little track, but we had managed to put enough dings and bruises on our bodies to make up for it. We crawled into the man-trip and groaned the whole way out. As Bobby and I separated at the bathhouse, he told me, "I think we're lucky to be alive." I replied that I thought he was right.

That night, in my bare little room at the Club House, I sat

on my bed and pondered things, and then I went outside into the night. I looked over my little town, and my eyes strayed to the Community Church, sitting prettily, its white steeple pointing toward the vast, starry sky. I was worried about the next day. We had done a terrible job. *Maybe*, I thought, *we should have said that prayer before we started to work.* And as soon as I thought that, all my aches and pains seemed to subside. *Is that it, Lord?* I thought. The Lord, if he heard, didn't say anything. I guess He doesn't have to if the answer is obvious.

The next morning, it was just Bobby and me again. "Let's pray!" I cried as soon as we got to our track.

"You got that right!" Bobby said. I guess he'd been pondering along the same lines as I.

I fumbled around until I came up with this: "Lord, whatever Johnny would have said for this section of track, you probably know what it's supposed to be. Bobby and I here could sure use your help. Oh, and let us work hard and do right by the company, too. Amen."

All day, work went as smoothly as if Johnny had been there. Afterwards, Bobby and I sat thoughtfully on the man-trip as we went out. "What are you thinking?" Bobby asked.

"I'm thinking maybe I don't know as much as I think I do."

"Amen," said Bobby.

The next summer, I worked in the mine again. This time, I didn't have Johnny or Bobby with me, but I remembered to pray. Each day, just as Johnny had taught, I asked God that I do right and give the company a good day's work. The work I had to do was hard enough. My job was to set timbers and work with the roof bolters down at the face where the continuous miners ground at the seam of coal. Raw roof was exposed in the process, and until it got supported, it was dangerous and could fall without warning. One day, when the big machine was being directed at a cut, I moved off to stand near a pillar. All of a sudden, I heard something pop behind me, and when I turned to look, I got a face full of coal. Then I was swimming in it. A shank of the pillar had collapsed. I was down beneath a pile of coal. I couldn't breathe. I struggled, but the coal was too heavy. Then it came to me, don't ask me why, that I'd started the day with Johnny's prayer. I had worked hard and done good as far as I knew how. The Lord would take care of the rest. Johnny had said so. Just thinking that gave me courage. I kept fighting.

Then I felt the burden of coal being lifted off me and hands grabbing my shirt and pants, dragging me out of the filthy pile. I spewed coal dirt out of my mouth, my ears and my nose. Men poured water out of their lunch buckets on my face. I turned over onto my hands and knees and coughed and hacked until I'd gotten as much coal dirt out of me as I could. When I was helped to my feet, I felt oddly heavy. Then I realized all my pockets were filled with coal. I started emptying them out. A sea of black faces surrounded me, all looking worried. The foreman came running. "We ought to take you out, Sonny," he said.

I told him I was fine and didn't want to go anywhere. I was thinking of Johnny. I was supposed to work hard and do good. The Lord would take care of the rest. I still had a shift to pull. I pulled it. I never felt so strong and brave.

We work hard, do right and let the Lord take care of
*   the rest.*
We trust in God but rely on ourselves.
We are not afraid.

OTHER VOICES: WE TRUST IN GOD BUT RELY ON OURSELVES

Strength in Love and Prayer
Melba Looney Shoun

Growing up in Coalwood's sister town, Caretta, as a daughter of a coal miner was a wonderful life, one that I would not trade and have learned to appreciate more with each year that I live. As most children raised there in the 1950s and '60s, I enjoyed life to the fullest. We were so rich, not by society's standards but rich with a life filled with love, smiles, hugs, kind words, truth, peace and dreams. We lived in the shelter of the good earth formed into giant mountains, which we assumed were playgrounds created by God just for us. There were thousands of trees, which provided nutritious treats of nuts and fruits, stick horses, a vine to swing from, or just a place to lie under and dream. Our imagination was our source of entertainment. I knew nothing but happiness and was unaware of all the things that could worry or upset me until one particular afternoon when the earth shook violently. My mother ran out of the house and just stood frozen. I was begging her to tell me what was wrong. Soon, I discovered my father had been hurt in the mine.

The hospital had a policy that didn't allow kids in the sick rooms, so when my mom and I went to visit, I had to wait on the lawn down below my daddy's hospital room window. I sat there and prayed just like he had taught me. Both Daddy and God knew how much I needed reassurance that he would get well. Although he was in pain and could hardly move, he had the nurses help him over to the window. When I looked up and saw him in his broken condition waving to me, I collapsed onto the cool, dark green grass in tears of relief and joy. Only then did I know for sure that God was answering my prayers and my daddy would soon be coming home.

The Miracle
Trula Vandell Gray

"John is such a good baby," my mother would say. "I can put him on the kitchen table while I clean and mop the floor, and he won't even move toward the edge." Then, right after New Year's Day in 1955, John got a bad cold. The doctor came to visit a neighbor's child, so Mom asked him to look at John. After examining the baby, the doctor said, "Mrs. Vandell, you need to take John to the hospital for some blood tests. I'm worried about his color." So John was admitted to the hospital for tests. It was found that John had one-sixth of the hemoglobin that he needed, and transfusions were begun in his ankles with Dad's donated blood.

While Mom was at the hospital with John on a Wednesday night, she observed pastors and Christian witnesses visiting patients in nearby rooms. She found herself pondering the Scriptures dealing with the woman who was healed from the "issue of blood," and she found herself wishing that someone would come and pray for John's "issue of blood." Suddenly there was a knock on the door, and a woman asked if they could come in and pray with her. Mom explained John's condition, and they began to pray for healing and comfort for John and for Mom. After the sincere, spirit-filled prayer, one of the visitors introduced himself as the pastor of a church in Nagutuck, Kentucky. He said, "I must explain how we came here to pray with you. You see, we sing on the radio and we were on our way to the radio station here. As we were driving up the hill near the hospital, the car stalled and it wouldn't start up again, no matter what we tried. We decided to pray, thinking that this was where the Lord wanted us to stop for some reason. As we prayed, the name Vondell or Van-something kept coming to me. So, we went into the hospital and asked if there was a man named Vondell here. The nurse said, 'No, but there's a baby here named John Vandell, and he's very sick.'"

The preacher went on to say, "So, Mrs. Vandell, the Lord sent us here to pray for your baby." As they left, Mom thanked the strangers from Kentucky, and she thanked God for His healing and comfort. The next morning as the doctor made his rounds at the hospital, he told Mom that John had anemia and that he would need to take liquid iron supplements to build up his hemoglobin. He added, "Mrs. Vandell, when I first examined your baby, I would have staked my reputation as a doctor that your baby had leukemia. I was that sure of it. Thankfully, it's anemia and can be treated." Mom thanked the doctor, but of course she knew who really to thank.

Washing Up the Lord
Kaye Wilkinson Price

I was born and raised a Coalwood girl. My father was a great-great nephew of Mr. Carter, who founded Coalwood. He was a self-taught mechanical engineer. My family lived in a big white house (#31) on the side of the hill down in what we called Middletown. One Sunday, when I was a very little girl, I took all the money I had—it was probably not much more than a dollar—to Sunday school. I was glad I did because Mrs. Chickos, my Sunday school teacher, said something that made me put every bit of what I had in the collection plate. When I got home, I ran to my mother and told her what I'd done. When she asked me why, I told her that Mrs. Chickos said that we needed to "Wash up the Lord with Tide and offerings." I had given all my money, I explained, so that Jesus could get a bath. My mother turned away and held on to the kitchen sink to keep me from seeing her laugh. The following week, she told Preacher Looney about me and the "Lord's bath." But he didn't laugh. He found me and took my face in his big hands so that I could see the sparkle in his eyes. He told me that I was a good person with a kind heart and Jesus would surely enjoy the wash-up just as He washed up our sins.

I don't remember the year, but one time Coalwood had a big flood. Coal boxes, wooden lawn furniture and walkways all were washing down the creek. My best friend, a girl named Margie Jones, and I were watching them float by. Then we got the bright idea that we'd like to float down with them. I think I had just finished reading *Huckleberry Finn*. Margie climbed on one of the coal boxes and started her

journey. I was at a bridge downstream to catch her as she
went by. But the coal box started to spin and sink before it got
there. I just barely managed to grab Margie's arms to drag her
out of the water, but the force of the water was too much for
me. I started praying for God to help me lift her out of the
water. All of a sudden, Garnet Crowder, a coal miner who
lived just down the street from us, appeared. "What are you
two crazy girls doing?" he demanded. Then he lifted Margie
to safety. He had a lot to say to the two of us and later to our
parents. Our parents took it from there. I have always
believed God sent Garnet Crowder out on his front porch
just in time to see Margie's wild "raft ride." I guess he didn't
want to see us get "washed up" the wrong way. Margie is still
my best friend, and we often laugh about that wild ride and
give thanks to both God and Garnet Crowder.

Let It Begin with Me
Linda Holder Alderman

When I think of growing up in Caretta and going to school
in Coalwood, my thoughts go back to when I took a few
piano lessons from a man blind from birth, Mr. Hatfield. He
was a relative of the Hatfields who fought the McCoys in the
famous feud, but there was never a more gentle man. He
was patient and loved teaching. The excitement of the
lessons was enhanced by the sweet smell of his cherry pipe
tobacco and the wonder of his immaculate cloth house slip-
pers, a rare sight in the coalfields.

I was raised to believe I could do anything. I said to my
mother, "If you will buy me a pair of skates, I can skate." The

next Christmas morning, I flew across the highly polished linoleum floors without a bobble. Hattie Holder was actually the best Christmas gift I had. She was a wonderful mother. Everyone felt her charm and warmth. She was saved at a revival in Buchanan, and soon after, I was, too. I still believed I could do anything, but it was enhanced by knowing the Lord.

Often I think of that old song we used to sing: "Let there be peace on Earth, and let it begin with me; let there be peace on Earth, the peace that was meant to be."

WE TRUST IN GOD BUT RELY ON OURSELVES: A SUMMARY

I firmly believe that the people of Coalwood had it exactly right when it came to religion. They believed in God but also believed that they had been given brains for a purpose, so that they and their children could understand more than what the preachers preached. They were certain that their Creator wanted them to contemplate the wondrous world through more than the glass of a religious doctrine. They looked for God everywhere. It helped them beat fear at every turn.

Every night when I was a very young boy, my mother would come into my room and hear my brother Jim's prayer and then mine. I said the prayer she taught me:

> *Now I lay me down to sleep,*
> *I pray the Lord my soul to keep.*
> *If I should die before I wake,*
> *I pray the Lord my soul to take.*
> *Amen*

It was a prayer that gave me courage. I was going to sleep, and it was all right, no matter what happened, because Mom said it was all right and God was going to be there with me. "That's my brave boy," she'd say when I was done. "Sleep tight," and so I did, certain of the ways of the universe and the Creator who'd constructed it. It's still a powerful prayer. Every so often, I'll still say it just before I go to sleep, just to touch the little boy I used to be and the God who's still there and hasn't changed.

Religions are designed to explain a Creator who cannot be explained. That is the glory of theologians and also their flaw. It is the same with science. Science attempts to explain how the universe is organized and to define the laws that seem to regulate it. But no scientist can truly explain the universe or its laws. They are ultimately unfathomable, and both a wise scientist and theologian understand that. It is beyond our human capacity to completely figure out the nature of God or the universe.

One of the most difficult things to explain is why there is goodness. Why, in a universe and a world where everything must work hard to simply survive, did that which we think of as decent and fine get embedded into our souls? Why is it that we crave goodness, seek out honesty and strive to be honorable even when evil is so much easier? How is it that evil, the desire to destroy and hurt others, hasn't been the driving force in our species and our world and our universe? Some great goodness is out there, and it's here, too. It is everywhere.

The people of Coalwood were good people, and they believed they'd been made to be that way. They were also made to be strong and intelligent, too. They were given strong bodies to work and sound minds to think, and they figured they'd best use them both to keep themselves and their families housed and clothed and fed and educated. For those among them who had not been given the same blessings, they did what they could for them as well. Coalwood's people did not make a habit of crying out "Lord, Lord!" They did the best they could do. God lived in their hearts, and just knowing that made them unafraid.

If you live in fear and are nagged by the voice of dread, take up the belief that there is a God of goodness who awaits you, filled with love and comfort. But to take the Coalwood model, it is wrong to accept that love and comfort without also using all the capabilities and possibilities you have been given. A human being is two parts, one spiritual and the other physical. Both are important. The design of the human body and mind is evidence of that great truth. We have to trust in the spirit that is everywhere around us and in us. But we also must use our hands and minds to keep our families safe and build a better world. That was the attitude of the people of Coalwood, and it helped make them the strongest, least fearful people I've ever had the privilege to know.

> *We trust in God but rely on ourselves.*
> *We are not afraid.*

The Coalwood Assumption

We are not afraid.

S ometimes now, there will be a trick of light or shadow, or maybe a sound or a smell, that will take me back to those days when I was a boy in Coalwood, West Virginia. Over the years, if I had been asked about my hometown, I might have replied that I knew every inch of the place, every smoky hollow and musical creek. I would have laughed and said I knew every miner who lived there, too, and his missus and their children, and even all the dogs and cats. I would have been certain that I had the place completely figured out in my mind, every curved road that led through the town as well as the crooked paths covered with pine needles that went up and over its forested hills. Like the beating of my own heart, I knew Coalwood's rhythms, punctuated by the low grumble of shuffling hardtoe boots as the shifts of miners treaded past my house to and from the tipple grounds of the Olga Number One mine.

But when you think you surely must know everything about a place, I think the truth is you don't really know it at all. To see it, you have to leave and then come back and look at it with different eyes. That's what happened to me when I began to write my Coalwood series, beginning with *Rocket*

Boys. I had different eyes then, older eyes, and I finally began to see Coalwood the way it really was. The strength and courage I recalled in its people were something of a surprise. During all the years after I'd left the town, I thought it had been just another place to grow up. How wrong I was. As I wrote about it, I was reminded by my own memories that Coalwood was a town filled with a good and honest people who had learned to conquer fear. And they had also taught me and all my childhood friends how to live a life unafraid.

I don't think it's much of a secret that I've done a lot of things during my life, had my share of adventures, been through a war, and got some medals. I've trained astronauts to go into space and taught hundreds of people how to scuba dive. I've dived down into deep, underwater wrecks for research and fun, and once I nearly got myself killed while trying to rescue people who had been trapped underwater. That was when a paddleboat sank in the Tennessee River and I went after the people inside. I was a minute too late. Although I got the people out, none of them survived. They gave me a medal for that, too, but I don't think I deserved it. But I did what I had to do and found the strength to do it.

During my life, it seemed to me that when things got particularly rough or frightening, I always discovered a little extra strength to keep going forward. Don't take me wrong. I've been scared a bunch of times. During the morning of the first day of the bloody 1968 Tet Offensive in Vietnam, I was so rattled I put my boots on the wrong feet and didn't notice it until I crawled exhausted into my tent that night. On a deep dive, I once went inside an upside-down wreck and, in an inky blackness illuminated only by my weak flashlight, discovered the remains of a dead crewman who wasn't supposed to be there. I came close to tearing out the side of that ship to get away. I sat on a truck in Tanzania one time and had a hungry lioness make eye contact with me. With a glance, she thoroughly intimidated me. She was sizing me up, and my heart beat pretty fast under her steely-eyed gaze. When I worked for NASA, I had to occasionally stand up in front of a lot of important people, sometimes including astronauts who had walked on the moon or flown for days through space, and explain some plan or design my office was proposing. That could fill my stomach with butterflies. After *Rocket Boys* was published, I was invited by West Virginia University to give the 1999 commencement address for its graduates. Dressed in a long, velvet gown and determined not to stumble, I entered a vast arena of cheering West Virginians. That was a bit daunting. It was the same when I went on my friend David Letterman's television show. Millions of people had their eyes on this old West Virginia boy, including my mother, a worrisome thought all by itself. Still, in all these situations and a lot more, and even when I was scared, I have persevered, certain that I had a reserve of strength that would get me through. It was only when I began to write my books about Coalwood that I realized that this confidence came not from me but from the people who had raised me. Their attitudes toward life had made them unafraid, and they had done their best to teach me and all the children I'd grown up with to live and think the same way.

In this book, I have tried to explain the strong and courageous attitudes of Coalwood's people so they might be used as a model for a life unafraid. To be truly free and happy, we must all free ourselves of the awful habits of fear and dread. To continue the journey to a fearless life past this book, I also recommend looking for other examples of people who have endured and prospered. This can include your parents, your friends and people you respect. Talk to them and listen carefully to their stories of how they have gotten past bad times, of the mistakes they've made, and how they've overcome them. Talk to a cancer survivor, a war veteran, a policeman or a fireman. When you do, you will rarely hear them speak of self-pity. They have endured and learned to be strong and happy. Listen closely and understand you are not the only person to face adversity, and if they can thrive, so can you. Understand that the world doesn't revolve around you, nor is it designed to hurt you. Be a dreamer, but also a doer. Rule fear and dread, not the other way around. Never doubt that you are part of a wondrous plan that requires you to do your part. Your Creator has given you the tools to accomplish so much, and you should get about doing it while living with strength and courage.

The despicable men who murdered thousands of innocent people at the World Trade Center and the Pentagon and aboard hijacked airplanes on September 11, 2001, were men who were ruled by fear. They woke up each morning dreading the world in which they lived and regretting who they were and how they fit into world society. They pitied themselves and became twisted by fear and regret until the only other emotion they could dredge up was hate. And so they killed as an expression of that hate. But other than murder, all they accomplished was to end their pathetic lives without ever truly living.

People who are tortured by fear don't usually commit

mass murder. Instead, they fail to better themselves, or tie themselves to jobs they despise, or join gangs, or turn cruel and bitter toward their spouses or children or friends. They become unable to enjoy life. Whatever you may do in the future, don't let yourself fall into this trap. Stay away from people who are always negative. They subtract from your life. That's why they're called negative. Talk instead to people who go about life in an optimistic way. Study them. Better yet, make them your friends. Adopt their attitude of living without fear and self-pity. Only then will you truly start living.

A few days after the murder of September 11, I boarded a jet plane and flew to New York City. A lot of my friends wondered why I would do such a thing since it was so dangerous. I told them I had business there, and I was going. I had thought about what my father would have done and concluded that if there had been important coal mine business to accomplish, and it required him to be on a jet plane, he would have been on it, no matter what. So I went. I was one of six passengers on a jumbo jet. One of them was a physician of Pakistani descent who had been stranded in Florida and was trying to make his way home. He was extremely nervous, both because he was afraid someone might mistake him for a terrorist and because he was afraid one of the other five passengers along for the ride might actually *be* a terrorist. I sat with him and we talked. Before long, we were talking about Coalwood and the people who raised me. And before long, he wasn't afraid. We laughed about the sometimes strange ways of the people who brought me up, but he saw their wisdom, straight and clear. I hope you do, too. Life is filled with risks, but the biggest risk, it seems to me, is to

live your life tied down by fear and dread. Life is too pre-
cious to lose a second of it being afraid. As Quentin, the
brains of the Rocket Boys, would say, life is *prodigious.*
Pursue happiness. That's your God-given right, along with
life and liberty. It says so, right there in our Declaration of
Independence.

When I was a boy, one of my favorite places to go was a
hollow high on the mountain behind my house. The hollow
was filled with tall pine trees and its floor was a plush carpet
of dropped needles. It was a place where the industrial song
of Coalwood subsided, and the only sound I could hear was
the wind rustling the tops of the pines or the squawk of the
occasional squirrel. I would often go there alone and sit on a
dead log and listen to nothing except the beating of my own
heart and the thoughts racing through my head. The old
green trees arched above and dusted me with their sharp,
fresh perfume and rustled their billowy skirts of fringed
boughs and preened a bit, it seemed to me, in the rarified
air. I loved that old hollow and those old trees. I was alone in
a deep wood, but I was absolutely, utterly at peace, completely unafraid. I wish every child in the world could have
such a place to go, where they could be safe and the world is
quiet and their parents wait nearby for them with patience
and love. If only the whole world could take on the attitudes
of the people of Coalwood, it could be so. Sometimes when
I imagine myself back in that hollow of pine, I wonder why
so many people choose to live harsh, ugly lives when all they
have to do to be happy is to be like the people of Coalwood,
honest and hard-working and free. I don't have an answer,
but I wonder about it all the same.

Coalwood has changed over the years. The bright, busy

town I knew while growing up no longer exists. My mother was right when she told me to build my rockets and go to college, that the town I loved was slowly dying. The coal mine at its center began its long decline in the early 1960s. Different companies bought and sold the mine, each becoming more and more detached from the town. No longer did the coal company finance schools, build ball fields, sponsor the annual Veteran's Day Parade float, produce the Christmas Pageant on the Club House lawn or subsidize the churches. No longer were men like my father around to sustain the Coalwood Proposition that guaranteed a man a good job as long as he gave a good day's work. The company in Coalwood became just another employer, and there wasn't much loyalty to it. Coalwood's mine finally closed on October 1, 1982. In a history of the town written just before he died, my father himself wrote the eulogy:

> *To those who have been a part of the coal industry for the last fifty years, the closing of Coalwood's mine was no surprise. The coal industry has always been a feast or famine situation. Coal will come back—it always has! But Coalwood, as I knew it, will not. It requires some imagination to see Coalwood as the people who built it saw it. There were no roads of any kind, no houses, nothing. But from nothing, the Carter family, Captain Laird and the other men of that time built a fine place to work and live. It became a bountiful place where a good life was in store for everyone who came there. The men of my generation carried their vision forward, and we built Coalwood into a place of pride. But we had our time, and now it is over. It was a good*

time, a wonderful time, when our miners were the best
in the world and our town the finest we could make it.
I only wish I had it to do all over again.

My father died of black lung in 1989 in Myrtle Beach, not in his beloved Coalwood. I still miss him. He was the bravest and finest man I've ever known. And he was right. Coalwood was never the same after its mine closed and most of the men and women who built it and raised my generation had gone. It became a shell of what it was, and many of its houses were abandoned. The old school was burned down by arsonists. The last vestiges of the mine itself were removed by the federal government and allowed to be hidden beneath encroaching vines and groves of rhododendron. Where once thousands of men had descended each day into the vast depths to gouge out the black diamonds so desperately needed by the other men who made steel, there were only faded signs, weeds and silence.

But Coalwood yet lives. When *Rocket Boys* was published and the movie *October Sky* came out, the town began a new life. Tourists arrived, wanting to meet the handful of people described in the books who are still there, like Bill Bolt, the machinist who built our rockets, or Red Carroll, Rocket Boy Jimmie O'Dell Carroll's father. They wanted to see and touch all the old places and just breathe in the air of the town that dreamed and accomplished great things. The people of Coalwood greeted the new visitors with warmth and hospitality. Soon, there was a small museum across from the house where I grew up, celebrating not only the Rocket Boys but Coalwood's mining heritage. The Cape Coalwood Restoration Association was formed by Coalwood residents, determined to rebuild the old rocket range and turn it into a park where families could go and remember rockets that once flew into the air, propelled not by physics but by the dreams of boys. They did all that and more, working hard with their own hands and money to restore as much of the town as they could. The state government began to pay attention to the visitors coming to see Coalwood, and it didn't take long before there wasn't a pothole to be found in McDowell County. The guest book kept at the museum soon boasted entries from people from nearly every state in the union and more than a dozen countries. Every year now, the townspeople hold an October Sky Festival. The other Rocket Boys and I attend, along with many of the other real-life people in the books and movie. Sometimes, my mom, now eighty-nine years old but still managing her life quite well, thank you, even puts in an appearance. Coalwood endures, as it always has, but with a new vigor and a new pride. A place where the old ways are still sacred, it still has much to teach us. Sometimes, I think maybe God just missed Coalwood. Perhaps that is why I was allowed to bring it alive again.

Maybe there was another reason, too. Maybe it was so I would get the chance to write down the wisdom of Coalwood's founders and builders at a time when so many people in our country so desperately need it. Maybe it was so I could recall for people who had taken on the habits of fear and dread that there is a better way.

> *We are proud of who we are.*
> *We stand up for what we believe.*
> *We keep our families together.*
> *We trust in God but rely on ourselves.*

These were the attitudes of strength and courage that sustained Coalwood's people through perilous times. Put together, it gave them an assumption about life that was their affirmation, not too often said aloud but understood deep within their souls:

We are not afraid.

On Flight 93, the aircraft that ended up crashing into a meadow in Pennsylvania on September 11, men and women stood up for themselves against monsters. They were proud of who they were, part of sturdy American families, and they trusted God but relied on themselves. They are heroes who will never die, not while any citizen of the United States of America still draws breath. They are part of who we are, and we are part of them, too. When they stood up, it was clear what they were saying to themselves, to their families and friends, to the morbid hijackers, to all of us:

We are not afraid.

We are not afraid. Say it slowly, and savor it. Know who you are. You come from a great people who built a magnificent civilization based on the principles of freedom and justice for all. From the Pilgrims who came ashore on the rocky beaches of New England, to the great, ancient tribes of brave and resourceful American Indians, to the men and women come from Africa, enslaved but willing to stand up for their freedom, to the last settler who pushed across the plains and snowy mountains to find a scrap of land on which he and his family could farm, and even to the astronauts who walked on the moon, we are a people who were often frightened but never gave up. We made mistakes, but because we are a free and fair people, we have always worked to correct those mistakes, to let everyone share in the freedoms for which so many of us so often died.

We are proud of who we are.
We stand up for what we believe.
We keep our families together.
We trust in God but rely on ourselves.

Take these attitudes as your own, and all will be well. There is no reason for you to fear life or dread what might be coming your way. Every hour of every day, recall all the people who came before you, all those who make up who you are, and stand tall and be proud. No matter how perilous the times, they will always be with you just as the people of Coalwood are always with me, whispering these truths: We are the people of a great nation. We have defeated every tyrant who ever tried to enslave us. We are Americans.

We are not afraid.

The Coalwood Attitudes of Strength and Courage

We are proud of who we are.
We stand up for what we believe.
We keep our families together.
We trust in God but rely on ourselves.

The Coalwood Assumption:

We are not afraid.

Appendix:
Questions for Homer

We Are Not Afraid presents and explains the attitudes that kept the people of Coalwood strong
during perilous times. By learning what sustained
them, I believe we can use their lessons as a model to live
good and happy lives in the world that changed forever on
September 11, 2001. Even before I wrote this book, the
Coalwood Trilogy (*Rocket Boys/October Sky, The Coalwood
Way* and *Sky of Stone*) prompted many people to write and
ask me questions about the best way to cope in today's stress-
filled and fearful world. Here are some of the best.

Q: I live in a big city, and my family is far away. It just
doesn't seem like I can meet or make friends, and I
hate being alone all the time. Life seems drab. If you
have any suggestions, I'd sure appreciate them.

A: First off, understand that being lonely is not abnormal. There are so many things that wall us off from other people—television, computers, movies, automobiles, etc. Coalwood people were always getting out and talking to each other and doing active things. It seemed to make them healthy and happy. You should do the same. Get away from the things that keep you indoors when you can and move into a more active lifestyle. Start accomplishing new things, whatever they may be. Develop a skill—like woodworking, auto repair, machine shop work. Or get involved with running, baseball, hiking, playing a musical instrument, swimming, building robots, scuba diving, whatever it may be as long as it gets you out and about and meeting other people. You also need to have a variety of experiences to talk about when you meet new people. Remember when you talk to people to really listen to them. Sometimes, the best way to make a friend is to not say much at all but just show an interest in what the other person is saying. People love that!

Q: My friends are always running me down. They run themselves down, too. They like to make fun of others, and nothing anybody does is right. How can I change them?

A: I don't know that you can. Maybe you just need other friends. People who are always negative are dangerous to have around. Their attitude is addictive and can make you into a negative person, too. Seek out friends who are doing good things and who think positively. Their attitudes are addictive, too, but that's a good thing!

Q: Since the September 11 terrorist attacks, my ten-year-old son has refused to fly. He gets hysterical when we bring it up. We really want to visit our family during the holidays as usual, but what can I tell him to help him not be afraid to get on an airplane? For that matter, I'm not sure I want to fly either. Any advice?

A: First off, when I was ten years old (or any age, including my present fifty-nine) I would have never told my mother that I was afraid to do something she wanted me to do. If I had, I'm certain she would have taken it as a challenge to think up something even worse! "Afraid to fly, are you, Sonny boy?" she would have said. "It must be the Hickam in you. We Lavenders aren't afraid of anything. But poor little baby, so afraid. How about I come to your school tomorrow and give you a big old hug and a kiss in front of God and everybody?" My response to *that* would have been to suggest she'd heard me wrong, that what I really wanted to do was to be tied to the wing of the airplane and flown upside down! Mom's psychology can work for you, too. No parent should ever give in to a child's fears. If you do, you only reinforce them. The way to handle expressions of unreasonable fear from a child about doing something normal (and flying these days is absolutely normal) is to respond to it with a matter-of-fact clarity that *it is going to happen.* "Mom, I'm afraid to fly!" "Go get the stuff you want to take to Grandma's." "Mom, I'm afraid to fly!" "Now, what did I do with that duffel bag?" And so on. I think you get the picture. Of course, this also presupposes that since the day he was born, your child has known that you are *not his friend.* You are *his parent.* What you say goes. I suggest you be a little eccentric, too, like my mom. Don't ever let a child be able to predict your response to any of their foibles. Let it vary, from milk and cookies to massive retaliation. As for you, an adult in the twenty-first century, saying you're afraid to fly: Get real. As the people in Coalwood used to say: "There's things a whole lot worse than dying, and one of them is not living free." If you don't take advantage of the wonderful opportunities that modern aviation provides, it's the same as going around in shackles. Aviation has opened up the world! *Go!* One more thing. The airlines of the United States are working hard to make their planes as safe as possible. They have the best safety record of any transportation system in history. Security is only going to get better. Cockpits are being secured, and crews are being instructed to never surrender their aircraft. Remember to also help yourself stay safe. Pay attention to what's going on around you. Know where to go and what to do in case of an emergency. And if you're ever aboard a hijacked airplane, fight back.

Q: My daughter is so unhappy at school. She is smart and funny, but is taller and skinnier than the rest of her ninth-grade classmates, and they find it great fun to torment her. They block her from her locker and say things like she's a lesbian or call her four-eyes. Why are kids so cruel? I am afraid this will scar her for life, and I feel so helpless and don't know how to help her.

A: You make it sound as if she's all alone, and maybe she is. That could be the real problem. It's usually the loners who get picked on, and if your daughter runs in a pack of one, that needs to change. I grew up a pretty puny kid. I wore thick glasses and had a lisp. I got picked on by a few bullies, but I had good friends, ones I knew I could count on. I was never unhappy at school, even when some kids were mean to me, because I had plenty of friends who I knew liked me. It sounds as if your daughter needs to get herself some good friends. Encourage her to find friends at school who are interested in the same things she is. To do that, she needs to be a joiner. Tell her to join everything. She'll find friends, and when she does, let her have them over for pajama or pizza parties. Get to know the other parents in your daughter's class, too. Be a big school supporter. And never, ever miss a PTA (or whatever they call the parent-teacher's organizations) meeting. You can also head off the problem of having an easily intimidated child by making sure he or she learns to be proud of who she is. Make sure she knows all about her family and is proud of you and those who came before. No matter where they go or what they do, as long as they know who they are and are proud of it, your kids are going to be fine. As for why children are cruel, I don't know. Not all of them are, of course. But there are always a few bullies around, and not all of them are kids! Be proud and strong, and stick with your friends, good and true. That's the best way to avoid bullying.

Q: I read where you said that one way to be unafraid is to be proud of who you are. But I'm adopted. How can I know who I am?

A: First off, you know you're a human being, the result of countless generations of men and women who survived some pretty tough times and got through them well enough to produce children. Otherwise, you wouldn't be here at all! By your address, I also see you're an American. That's really about all you need to know. Study your American history, and you'll be proud of who you are right there! But someone who is adopted should also be proud of their adoptive parents and all those who came before them as well. After all, your parents didn't have to have you. They chose you, and because they've raised you, you're part of them, too. Even for those folks who can trace their lineage all the way back to the Pilgrims, their gene pool has become huge over time with thousands of other family members. So honor your adopted parents. Find out who they are by asking them to tell you stories of their youth and of their parents and as far back as they go. Then be proud that you got asked to join their club!

Q: When I was young, I used to dream about being an astronaut or just working for NASA. Now, I'm over thirty years old and I'm stuck in a job I hate. Is it too late to go after my dream? Also, changing careers is a huge step that I think I might be afraid to do. Where can I find the courage to do this?

A: I was thirty-eight years old before I started to work for NASA. I always had a passion for space and kept my eye on my goal even after being rejected time after time when I applied. To reach your dream, no matter what it is, you've got to first figure out how to do it. This gets into my three Ps of success—passion, planning and perseverance. Simply put, when you have a passion for something, get a plan, then follow it and never quit. I don't think it's ever too late to accomplish great things. As for the courage to change your career, consider the harm that working in a job you hate is doing to you and your family. It's not a matter of being happy. It's a matter of reaching your potential. It is corrosive to your mind, your heart and your soul to spend a lifetime doing something you don't like. Be mindful of your family when you contemplate changing your career. If you have taken on a family, your first responsibility is to keep it together. That's a sacred duty. Get them on your side. Make your dream their dream, too. Then go after it with everything you've got!

Q: Was there ever a time you felt like giving up? If so, what kept you going?

A: I guess I've thought about giving up, but I sure never made it a habit. As my mother said to my brother and me in *The Coalwood Way,* "You boys don't know a thing about quitting. I guess you haven't seen enough of it to learn." People in Coalwood hardly ever quit anything once they started. They thought it was bad for their character and a poor example for their kids, too. Just recalling the tough people who raised me is enough to get me going when I think I can't go on. You might want to read my Coalwood trilogy to get some inspiration.

Q: Why should we spend our tax dollars on space when the poor are hungry? Or when we need money to defend our country? Or we need to build roads? Or when I need help with medical bills? Isn't it just throwing away money for nothing?

A: First, let me make it clear that I don't buy into the argument that everything in the world should be done before we go into space. That's shortsighted thinking. If our ancestors had waited until they had all their problems solved before heading across the ocean, we'd have no country. But we do have a country, and it's a great one. I think to stay great, however, a country needs to accomplish great things, and it also needs a greater purpose. This is especially true of the United States. This is a country that does best if it has an eternal frontier to push up against. I believe our greater purpose should be to conquer and settle the solar system. The nice thing about that is the solar system is a very rich place, filled with not only mineral wealth but energy, a nearly inexhaustible supply. If there's one thing this country and this planet desperately needs, and is willing to pay for, it's energy. But going into space will always be more than acquiring energy and making money. It is also the place to discover where we fit in the universe. NASA's space telescopes and deep space probes are telling us more about our world and our solar system than we've ever known. In the past ten years, we've accumulated more knowledge about the universe than in all the years before. That's worth spending some tax dollars for! Recently, I was talking to some NASA engineers about the agency and why it was important to keep going, even during times of war, including this war against terrorism. I told them that NASA is needed to hold aloft the beacon of hope and inspiration. All wars end eventually, and when this one does, NASA must be there, still the best of the best, still consisting of the kind of people who will provide the true victory of taking the dreams of all mankind and making them come true. That, I believe, is NASA's duty, and I'm confident the men and women of the space agency will not fail.

Q: It just seems like America has no joy anymore. I think about what happened on September 11 all the time and worry for myself and my family constantly. We stay home from large groups now and are careful with the mail and won't even consider traveling anywhere. I watch or listen to the news all day, and it frightens me so. What else can I do to protect my family?

A: The best way to protect your family may be to turn off the television and radio. Keep this in mind. News organizations want you to pay attention. If you don't, they get taken off the air. Over the years, they've discovered people will tune in to bad news. Bad news equals big ratings. So the newscasters are naturally going to give out the worst news they can, and give it over and over. They beat that negative drum, and they're very good at doing it with suave announcers and colorful graphics. The more you hear of their negative drumbeat, the more negative you get yourself. Soon you're scared to death, but you can't quit watching and listening! But you have to. This isn't to say you shouldn't pay attention to the news. It's your civic duty to keep up with what is going on in your country and your world. But just remember to look around from time to time and notice that it's actually quite peaceful where you are. The birds are singing, children are playing, and the sun is shining. Stop constantly shouldering the problems of the world and go outside and enjoy life.

Q: I am a teacher, and I have such a hard time getting support from the parents. It seems they want me to raise their children, yet the rules are so tight now that I cannot hug a student to congratulate them or discipline them when they misbehave. I work so hard to give them the skills they need to move up in their studies and have a good life, but I am never thanked and barely can afford my modest house on my salary.

A: Here's what I believe: Teachers are the true heroes in this country, especially tough teachers who fight to make certain their students learn. Teaching, I believe, is a life-and-death situation. When I wrote about Miss Riley in *Rocket Boys* and *The Coalwood Way,* I made it clear that she believed that if her students didn't learn, they were doomed to a lifetime of ignorance, which meant poverty and depression and probably an early death. She was willing to fight against anyone who tried to keep her from doing her job. Like Miss Riley, I believe that you and all teachers must stand up and fight. That takes courage, but you must find it. If your unions are not interested in helping you, then you have to throw your union leaders out. Organize. Form associations with other tough teachers. Fight to bring discipline back into schools, and go out on strike to get some sense back into your lesson plans. Join political groups to get the school boards on your side. If you fight, you'll find that there are a lot of parents out there who will help you. Just let them know what they can do. There will also be a lot of parents who will oppose you and who will take you to court when you try to apply common sense to your teaching (which may mean the occasional whack in the seat of the pants of an unruly child). Being organized can counter that. Being organized means you have an organization that will line up with you in court and help pay your legal fees. Organization is the key. And never quit. It's the only way to save your students.

Q: I married at age twenty to my first girlfriend, and we have two young children now. Life is pretty dull, just the kids' soccer games and lawn mowing it seems. I see my unmarried friends and it seems they have no concerns and such a fun life that I wish I did too. I am considering a divorce while the kids are still young, but I am feeling a bit guilty and selfish.

A: You *should* feel guilty and selfish. I also guarantee you'll feel worse if you get a divorce and see what it does to your kids. I also suspect that your single friends often envy you when they return to their empty apartments at night and spend long weekends alone. The people of Coalwood who raised me believed that once you started a family, you never gave up on it. It was a sacred duty to keep it going. But they also were certain that being in a family was the best and happiest way to live. You need to develop a little pride in your family. Look upon it as a dynasty, something you'll build that will last forever. Make your family your passion. One thing I know. A child with divorced parents is going to feel insecure a good part of the time. So stay together, but for goodness sake, don't gripe and groan about it. Use your minds to figure out how to make your life together more interesting. Tolstoi said, "All happy families resemble one another; every unhappy family is unhappy in its own fashion." I would like to add one more sentence to that thought: *An unhappy family headed by interesting parents is worth the trouble.*

Q: I love reading about your father in your books. I was wondering if you might share a bit more about your relationship with him. What's your favorite memory? What was he like when you went to college? Was he still alive when you began working for NASA?

A: The most special moment between my father and me was, of course, our moment at Cape Coalwood when he finally came to see my rockets fly. He was most impressed with their design, and when the last one flew, *Auk XXXI*, he was the one who pushed the button to launch it. He became so excited that he began to dance. My father was usually very controlled, but the sight of that big old rocket splitting the sky filled him with a spirit I'd never seen! Dad's thoughts on my college years is explored thoroughly in *Sky of Stone*. Let's just say he wished I studied a little harder! In later years, I had two special moments with Dad I can recall. He came to Huntsville, Alabama, to visit me, and I took him out to NASA to see where I worked. He was very impressed with the Spacelab, a module that fit in the back of the space shuttle to carry science experiments. I had a hand in its design, so that made me proud. Later, he got to read *Torpedo Junction,* my first book, and pronounced it "very well researched." I considered that high praise from my dad!

Q: I had a very harsh father and wish I could be closer to him. You seemed to have the same problem with your father. Any advice on how I can change things between my father and me?

A: In many ways I wrote *Rocket Boys* for the generation of kids who had parents who came out of the Depression and World War II. Many of the fathers of that generation were never particularly close to any of their children, not just their sons. It's just the way they were. They went to work and made money, and their wives raised the kids. End of story. Still, even though my father was nearly always at work in the mine, I never doubted he loved me. My Coalwood trilogy of books explain so much more. I hope you can find it in your heart to forgive your dad. I bet he loves you very much but just doesn't know how to show it. Just honor him and, every so often, thank him for the things that he did for you, even if it was only to buy your schoolbooks. I think you'll find yourself a happier person.

Note: If you would like to write and tell me how you overcame the habits of fear and dread, please go to *http://www.homerhickam.com* and click on the *We Are Not Afraid* button. I look forward to reading your stories of strength and courage. They might just end up in one of my future books!

Questions for Homer from Young People

Q: The other kids in my class are constantly criticizing me. They make me feel so stupid. What helped you stay positive and focused when you were in school?

A: I was always a bit small growing up, mainly because I started school when I was a year younger than everybody else in my class. I also wore thick glasses, liked to read a lot and was the mine superintendent's son. Being the son of the "boss" can be hard. Still, I was a pretty popular kid! The reason was that I just let the mean things kids said about me roll off my back. I knew, in the long run, it didn't much matter. I was who I was, and that was that. There was no use worrying about it or getting mad when somebody said something. In fact, I kind of pitied kids who would say mean things to me because they couldn't see what a neat little guy I was! I wasn't afraid to stand up for myself either. Sometimes, you have to do that, not violently but at least toe-to-toe with someone who simply will not let you alone. Remember, there's always a tomorrow. If you get really, really mad, that's the time to do absolutely NOTHING. Let things cool down. You have lots of days in front of you. Someday, you will excel and the bullies will be left behind in the dust. Maybe you'll even be their boss! Sometimes, the best thing to do is to simply smile. And when somebody makes a joke at your expense, laugh and shake your head as if you've heard it all. That drives bullies and mean people crazy! Remember, you are YOU, and they don't get any better than that.

Q: Could you tell me more about your three "P's" for a happy and successful life?

A: The three "P's" are Passion, Planning and Perseverance. Those were the elements of success for the Rocket Boys in my memoirs. We loved to build rockets. It was our passion! Passion is a very important element in being successful. If you don't care about it, you're not going to be happy doing it. Let's say, just as an example, your parents think you should be a medical doctor but you'd rather be a paleontologist, someone who studies dinosaurs and fossils. You have a passion for that but you know you'd make a lot more money as a doctor. My experience is that money and recognition will come if you're passionate about what you do, no matter what it is. So you need to let your parents know and your teachers, too, that you'd really, really rather be a paleontologist, but not just any paleontologist—a famous dinosaur-hunter like Jack Horner or Mark Goodwin! Be enthusiastic about it! Passionate! And take positive steps to prove how serious you are about it! Go to a museum or a college and find someone who collects fossils and ask him or her how to get involved. Figure out how to go into the field and work with some real paleontologists and fossil-hunters. Be willing to walk for miles and dig for days! Show your enthusiasm. Then move into the second element of success: planning. You have to plan out how to reach your passion or you'll never make it. Let your parents and teachers and your new friends in the paleontology field help you. They can recommend the education you need to reach your life's passion and help you come up with a plan. Finally, there's perseverance, as important as the first two. I know many talented people who failed to reach their passion in life because they just didn't stick to it. I was thirty-eight years old before I got a job with NASA. And I was fifty-four years old before one of my books hit #1 on the *New York Times* Bestseller list. Perseverance, perseverance, perseverance! You have to go after your dream with all you've got for as long as it takes!

Q: I am a senior in high school. I live in a small rural area. I find it hard to have close friends because no one really has the same serious interests that I have, like computers or physics. You have lived though many problems that I have, as well as ones I haven't even thought of yet. I just wondered what you do to cope with loneliness and stress.

A: I was the only one of the Rocket Boys who was really interested in rockets and space. The others saw it as either a way to change their lives or to help me do what I wanted to do. We boys had always been very close. If any of them had expressed an interest in something, I would have helped them do what they wanted to do. I think that's the key. If you want friends, you have to be willing to show an interest in what they like to do and prove your friendship in that way. After you make a friend, they'll probably respond by showing a similar interest in what you like to do. Of course, programming computers is essentially a solitary process, one that tends to be done by only one person at a time. It is also very time-consuming. I used to program computers myself in several languages—FORTRAN, COBAL, BASIC, etc. You should probably limit yourself to a fixed number of hours per day in front of your computer. Look around. What else at your school might be interesting and allow you to be with others? Perhaps acting in a school play or being on the school newspaper staff? Those can be fun things to do, and you get to meet other kids, interact with them and build friendships. Remember, there is nothing more important in life than your friends and family. You need to build friendships and family relationships first and foremost. Without your friends and family, life will be empty. I've discovered most people will respond to you positively if you give them a chance, even people you thought didn't like you.

Q: Do you feel it's important for kids to have a positive role model?

A: You bet I do. Just make sure your role model is someone who's doing something good with his or her life. I fully understand why so many young people idolize popular rock musicians and movie stars. Their images are extremely strong, and they have powerful, rich organizations behind them. But one thing you should know is that most of those "stars" are actually extremely fragile personalities who tend to fall apart when they lose their popularity. They're nice to listen to or watch, but the person you see on stage or the screen isn't actually who they really are. Some of them also bring negative messages just because the more shocking they are, the more publicity and attention they get. In the end, a role model should simply be a good and honest and decent person. If possible, it's best to make yours someone you want to be like when you grow up, someone who is really happy in what they do. I recommend making your parents or one of your teachers a role model. They're someone you see every day!

Q: I'm afraid I'll never learn all the things I need to graduate from high school. Homework is a drag and so hard it takes me hours and hours every night to do it. Did you have trouble in school?

A: Oh gosh, did I have trouble in school! I just couldn't make good grades no matter how hard I tried. That is, until I started building rockets in high school. After I found this passion for space and rocketry and had a reason to learn a lot of things, it all became easy, even math and science. If a subject is difficult, be sure to tell somebody. Tell your parents and your teacher that it is hard for you, and let them know you're trying. Maybe you can do something extra to make up for poor test scores. A lot of us simply don't do well on tests, but that doesn't mean we're stupid! I made far worse grades than a lot of students in my class, but I ended up being a rocket scientist and a bestselling author! This is where perseverance comes in. Never give up! And please don't let anybody ever put you in a class that's for "slow learners." You're better than that! Buckle down and show everybody you deserve to be with the best because you ARE the best! One time I told my wonderful high school physics teacher Miss Riley that I was doing my best. She summed up her philosophy in two words: "Do better!" I've tried to follow her advice ever since.

Q: In the movie *October Sky,* I notice you dropped out of school to work in the coal mines. What advice would you give someone who was considering dropping out of school?

A: Simple. Never, never, *never* quit school! In fact, never quit *anything* you start! I tried to argue the director of *October Sky* out of that scene about me quitting school because it never happened. My parents would have lived in a tree before they would have ever let me quit school. They knew very well the value of a good education. Both of them were high school graduates, but they had gone as far as they could go. They were bound and determined that my brother and I would go to college. Getting a good education is the difference between a happy and an unhappy life. No one can ever learn enough! Make that your goal, to learn new things. Right now, I'm into dinosaurs. Last summer, I was with a team in Montana and we found a tyrannosaurus rex, and I was able to identify it because I recognized the toe bone of a big theropod (meat eater). I only got interested in dinosaurs a couple of years ago, and I didn't know one bone from another. Now, I'm getting pretty good at identifying them, and it's so much FUN! Learning new stuff is great!

Q: Do you feel that it's important for young people to ask for help from others in achieving their goals?

A: Sure I do. The great thing about living in the United States is that there are so many people who want to help young people. So let them help you! It makes them feel good to do it, and you'll actually be helped, too. This includes parents, teachers, club leaders, businesspeople, preachers, priests, rabbis, friends and so many others. And if you're a little shy because you think you're too different, that maybe you're the wrong race or gender or whatever, forget it! You live in a great nation that takes care of its own. Be a patriot. Don't listen to those who would run your country down. This is a great place, and with your help, it'll get even better. Remember, you have a right to be happy. It's right there in our Declaration of Independence. We have a right to life, liberty and the pursuit of happiness! If you're reading this and you're not in the United States, there are plenty of opportunities for you, too. All you've got to do is to look for them.

Q: Sometimes I worry that if I develop anything great some day it might lead to the corruption and demise of our own society. I am just asking for your advice.

A: Don't worry. Societies rise and fall, usually on their own merits. It's all a slow process. Just do what it is that interests you, is fun, but also keep in mind how it might help other people and your country, too. Do volunteer work when you can, something that allows you to work directly with other people. Build relationships. It's called networking. It will make you happier than you can imagine and also be good for your career.

Q: I pray to God almost every day, but yet He seems not to exist.

A: I think God has put the teenaged years on us as a special challenge. They used to say in Coalwood that God looks after fools, drunks, the United States of America and the Rocket Boys. He looks after you, too. Do you want to see a miracle? Look in the mirror. The odds of you being alive on this planet has more zeros than the stars themselves. Life is the greatest gift in the universe. Enjoy it. The second you aren't enjoying it, change what you're doing. Be creative to find joy. You have a right to be happy and also a responsibility to be happy.

Q: I feel like I am in a cold river. I am losing sight and direction in my life. I don't want to live like this anymore. Please help me.

A: Ultimately, you have to help yourself, as I know you're quite capable of doing. Whenever you find yourself down, look for anything to make you laugh, no matter how silly it is. And read. *Read every day.* Reading is the key to a good life. Right now, it seems wise for you to read things that are humorous, that will give you joy. Try reading Dave Barry's books, for instance. They're funny! Also, see if you can do one thing every day that will make somebody else smile. Take it as a special challenge. See how creative you can be. A smile that you've made happen can light up the darkest day.

Q: My friend wrote all of his friends a good-bye e-mail and committed suicide. He was depressed, but we never thought he would really do it. It has been a month, but everything seems so empty, and I am having a hard time concentrating at school.

A: I'm sorry to hear about your friend and hope you've gone to someone you respect and admire to talk to about it. If you haven't, please do so right away. Your friend needed help badly but decided not to work on his problems. Suicide, when you get down to it, is a very selfish act. Teen suicide is especially tragic, because it is so needless. Whatever is bothering a teenager will disappear as they get older. It will all pass, I swear!

Q: What do you consider your greatest personal achievement? What do you hope to accomplish in the future?

A: I hope I haven't accomplished my greatest personal achievement! It would be awful to think that everything I might do in the future is going to be less than I've already accomplished. Still, to date, I guess the best thing I've done is to write my Coalwood books and see the movie *October Sky* made. The reason that's important to me is because it resulted in the rebirth of Coalwood, my hometown. Can you imagine growing up in a little town, seeing it all but die, and then, because of something you've done, watch it come alive again? That's pretty amazing.

Q: Any other advice about staying positive and achieving goals?

A: You get one chance to make it a good life. That means you better make it a fun and happy life. In fact, the way I figure it, that's your job. The odds of anyone existing is trillions upon trillions to one. Think about it. In order for you to exist, everything that has ever happened had to occur exactly as it did to allow you to exist. Wow! The odds against you being here are so huge you couldn't come up with enough zeroes to describe it. But here you are. That means you are vastly special, no matter what! And you've been given a brain, too. Why do you think that is? It's so you can figure out how you can lead a joyful, useful, inspiring life. In my book *The Coalwood Way*, I write about how when I was a teenager, I suddenly found myself completely, utterly and totally "sad," but I couldn't figure out why I felt that way. Finally, I turned to my pal Quentin, and he got me thinking until I figured out what was bothering me. If you find yourself kind of sad and depressed from time to time, you might want to read *The Coalwood Way*. It's got some good things in it for you!

Note: If you would like to write and tell me how you overcame the habits of fear and dread, please go to *http://www.homerhickam.com* and click on the *We Are Not Afraid* button. I look forward to reading your stories of strength and courage. They might just end up in one of my future books!

About the Author

Homer Hickam has led a remarkable life. Not only is he a #1 *New York Times* bestselling author and the subject of the wonderful film *October Sky*, he's a former National Aeronautics and Space Administration (NASA) engineer with international accolades for his work, a scuba instructor who has led expeditions to sunken wrecks, a pilot, an amateur paleontologist, a decorated combat veteran and a renowned inspirational speaker. His books are being studied in over four hundred schools and colleges. And he's not done yet. Homer is a prolific writer who continues to write intriguing page-turners that are eagerly anticipated by his legions of fans.

During his long NASA career, Homer worked in propulsion, spacecraft design and crew training. His specialties at NASA included training individual astronauts on operating science experiments in space and extravehicular activities in space suits. He also trained astronaut crews for many Spacelab and space shuttle missions, including the hubble Space Telescope deployment mission, the first two hubble repair missions, Spacelab-J (he trained the first Japanese astronauts) and the Solar Max repair mission. Prior to his retirement from NASA in 1998, Homer was the payload training manager for the International Space Station Program.

Homer is the recipient of many awards and citations, including the Bronze Star and Army Commendation medals for his service in Vietnam, the coveted Silver Snoopy award for support of the astronauts, the NASA Marshall Space Flight Center Director's Commendation Award, the Alabama Distinguished Service Award for Heroism (for the attempted rescue of the passengers and crew in a paddleboat sinking), the Distinguished West Virginian Award, the Distinguished Virginia Tech Alumni Award, the National Space Club Media Award, and many, many more. He was also honored to be an Olympic Torch runner for the Atlanta Olympics. His book *Rocket Boys* was named by the *New York Times* as one of the Notable Books of 1998 as well as being nominated by the distinguished National Book Critics Circle for best biography of that year. All of his books have been national bestsellers.

Homer is married to Linda Terry Hickam, an artist and his first editor and assistant. They have four cats and live on a beautiful north Alabama mountain.